Dan Archer was born at Brookfield Farm, Ambridge, on 15 October 1896. During the First World War he served for two years in the 16th Battalion, The Borsetshire Regiment, but otherwise he has spent his entire life as a farmer.

In 1921, he married Doris Forrest, the daughter of a gamekeeper on the local estate, and they had three children – Jack, who became landlord of the village pub 'The Bull' and who died in 1972; Phil, who now runs Brookfield Farm with the help of his own son, David; and Christine, who is married to the present gamekeeper on the local estate.

In 1980, Doris died. Dan now lives alone (but with his family and friends in the village around him) at Glebe Cottage, and still takes a lively interest in the farming at Brookfield.

The Ambridge Years

DAN ARCHER

By arrangement with the British Broadcasting
Corporation

SPHERE BOOKS LIMITED

First published in Great Britain by
Michael Joseph Ltd 1984
Copyright © William Smethurst and Anthony Parkin 1984
Published by Sphere Books Ltd 1986
27 Wright's Lane, London W8 5SW
Reprinted 1986

TRADE
MARK

Set in 10 on 11pt Linotron Times

Printed and bound in Great Britain by
Cox & Wyman Ltd, Reading

Dedicated to the 'rising generation' – my great-grandchildren, Adam, Debbie, John, Helen, Tommy, James and little Kate.

PREFACE

Dan Archer's memories of farming in Ambridge in days gone by were first written down by his granddaughter Jennifer, who lives at Home Farm, Ambridge, with her husband Brian and her three children. Jennifer writes a weekly column in the *Borchester Echo*, and it was there that some of Dan's anecdotes first appeared. Several chapters of this book – including Dan's account of boyhood Christmases at Brookfield, the 'ploughing-in' at Weston Farm, and the Ambridge Fête between the wars – have previously been printed in the *Borchester Echo* and are included here by kind permission of the Editor.

CONTENTS

PREFACE   *page vi*

OCTOBER   *page 1*

NOVEMBER   *page 19*

DECEMBER   *page 37*

JANUARY   *page 54*

FEBRUARY   *page 69*

MARCH   *page 83*

APRIL   *page 97*

MAY   *page 112*

JUNE   *page 126*

JULY   *page 139*

AUGUST   *page 152*

SEPTEMBER   *page 165*

INDEX   *page 179*

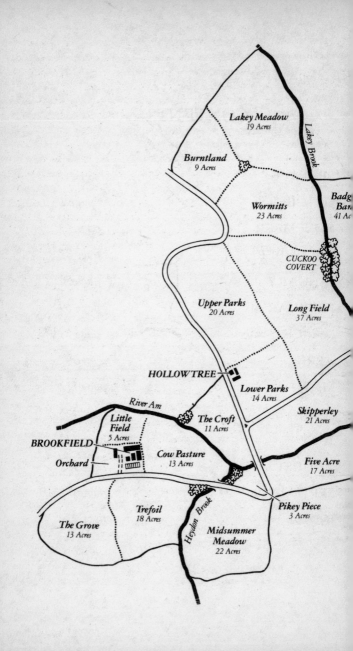

Brookfield Farm

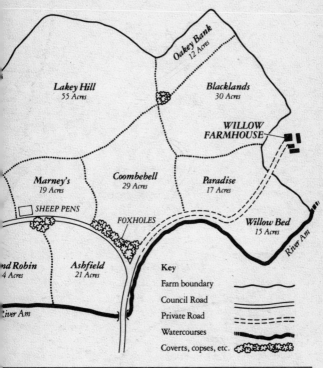

Oakey Bank
12 Acres

Lakey Hill
55 Acres

Blacklands
30 Acres

WILLOW FARMHOUSE

Marney's
19 Acres

Coombebell
29 Acres

Paradise
17 Acres

SHEEP PENS

FOXHOLES

Willow Bed
15 Acres

River Am

nd Robin
4 Acres

Ashfield
21 Acres

River Am

Key

Farm boundary	
Council Road	
Private Road	
Watercourses	
Coverts, copses, etc.	

tocking		Cropping	(Approx acreage)	Labour
Dairy cows	110	Wheat	100	Phil
Young stock	85	Barley	100	David
ows	60	Oilseed rape	50	Graham (cows)
wes	300	Potatoes	16	Neil (pigs)
		Grassland	242	Jethro (general)
		Total	508	
		plus buildings, roads, copses, etc.		

OCTOBER

I WAS born on 15 October 1896, during what countryfolk used to call 'St Lukes's Little Summer', because, around St Luke's Day, there is often a period of settled weather, when the sun shines with renewed warmth and the air is crisp and dry. It has always been a favourite time of year for me. When I was a small boy I liked it because I had a cake with candles and a new pair of boots to set me up for the winter. Then, in a lifetime of farming, I liked it because the calm, dry weather gave me a chance to press on with the ploughing and drill my wheat before nature shut up shop for the season.

Now that I'm retired, an old man living in a cottage, I find pleasure in just sitting in my garden chair, watching the sycamores change colour in the churchyard and the clouds of butterflies and bees as they weave and hum round the Michaelmas daisies. At night, too, at this time of year, I sometimes look out of my bedroom window, across the river to Brookfield land, and see the newly ploughed fields with a faint mist over them, all lit up by a hunter's moon. That's when I think back to the days when I was behind the plough and, before then, to my father's time.

Just an old man rambling over the fields of memory, but it's about the only thing an 'old man' is allowed to do these days. I'd like to see our Phil's face if I said I wanted a go on his £40,000 combine!

The first October day I can recall was my third birthday, in 1899. My mother was friendly with Mrs Gabriel, the blacksmith's wife, who brought her son Walter round to tea. Walter's cousin came as well with his wooden elephant called Buller, named after the famous general in the Boer War. We were in the orchard and he was pulling General Buller along. I tried to take it off him, it being my birthday after all, but he gave me a terrible thump and made my nose bleed. Great splashes of crimson coursed down my cream cotton blouse, redder and brighter than the Blenheim apples that were ripening all around us.

It was a useful lesson in life, not to try to steal wooden elephants off blokes older and bigger than yourself, and I daresay I benefited from it. A few months later came another experience concerning the war in South Africa, and very puzzling it was too. It must have been about ten o'clock one night when my father ran up the stairs into the bedroom where I was sleeping with my younger brother Ben, shouting: 'Mafeking's relieved! Mafeking's relieved!'

Well, I was very pleased to hear it, of course, and I think I shouted 'Hooray!' but I was puzzled all the same. Who on earth was Mafeking? And why was he so relieved? And what on earth was all the fuss about?

Not that it really mattered. It was enough that Ben and I were carried downstairs and given mugs of hot milk by our mother, who was heavily pregnant with my second brother, Frank, and very annoyed with my father for waking us up. We sat bundled up by the kitchen fire, wide-eyed, watching my father drink best October-brewed ale with George Atkins and another farmer who had ridden over with the news.

I don't know where my grandmother was that night. As it was past ten o'clock she'd have been tucked up in bed like me and Ben, I daresay. Perhaps she was too old to be excited by the marching of armies in distant lands, or perhaps (because she was more than a bit deaf) she was still asleep, unaware and forgotten as she snored her head off through the night of national jubilation.

She was a wicked old woman though, was Grandma. We boys knew it just about from the moment we were born. Who else would dare shout at my father and call him a daft 'fit for nothing' beggar when he lost a calf after struggling in the cowshed all night? Or refuse to curtsy to the new lady of the manor, young Lettie Lawson-Hope, when she came to Brookfield with a gift of cakes after my mother gave birth to Ben? It became a famous family story, that did. 'I noticed, Mrs Archer, that you did not curtsy to me when I came in,' said young Lettie, and Grandmother replied: 'I bow my knee to God Almighty and God Almighty alone!'

Poor Lettie Lawson-Hope! She had only just married the Squire and didn't even know that while her nourishing cakes were welcomed by cottagers, they were a bit of an insult to a family of yeoman farmers.

It was Grandma, I remember, who thrust me out of the warm kitchen on a chill October morning and told me not to come back until I'd found her some late mushrooms in the paddock for her breakfast. And it was Grandma who terrified me when I was eating some fat, juicy blackberries by telling me the devil had spat on them on Michaelmas Day. But it was also Grandma, I have to admit, who taught me many of the old country names of flowers, like 'Butter-and-Eggs' for toadflax, 'Angels Eyes' for speedwell, and 'Kiss-me-Quick' for tansy.

My earliest memory of all, I think, was when I was two years old and my mother was confined with Ben. Grandma took me down to the village and dumped me at the school for the morning while she went to visit friends. Lost, bewildered and terrified, I was hauled around the school field at dinnertime by a gaggle of huge, giant-sized girls of six or seven, who made me howl by linking hands and singing the old children's rhyme:

> Broad beans and butterflies,
> Tell me when your mother dies,
> I'll begin to bury her,
> Broad beans and butterflies,

3

But I was three when Grandma did what I thought at the time was the wickedest thing of all. My mother had perched me at the kitchen table one afternoon with a plate of bread and butter in front of me and had gone off, carrying little Ben, to feed the hens. Grandma was sitting by the range and I gradually realized, to my horror, that she was taking sheets out of a large box and tearing them up into long, thin strips. At first I stared at her, my bread and butter forgotten, scarcely able to believe my eyes. Then I shouted at her sternly, telling her to stop, but she just gave me an evil grin and tore another linen sheet right down the middle. That was when I bawled to my mother, fearful, even at that early age, that I would somehow be blamed for such a terrible domestic tragedy. Mother came running back, startled by my yells, and explained that Grandma was not venting her known spite on us all, but was making bandages for 'our boys that were out'.

The truth about Grandma was, I believe, that she found us a dull lot. She had married my grandfather, Daniel William Archer, because he cut a dashing figure in a black stovepipe hat and a pirate's beard. She had brought him six silver spoons and £700 and, to everyone's surprise, she didn't mind one bit when Daniel William blew most of the money in the first year. That was back in the early 1850s, when £700 was a lot of money, so goodness knows what my grandfather managed to spend it on around Borchester. There can't have been much in the way of dancing girls, I don't suppose champagne was more than a bob a bottle, and he wasn't a gambling man. I still have three of the spoons, engraved with 'JS,' the initials of Josiah Simms, and beautiful they look too when they're polished up. The Simms of Little Croxley were farmers in their own right, owners of broad acres, and they had a piano in their parlour which in those days meant a great deal.

What Grandma (or the young, eighteen-year-old Elizabeth Harriet Simms as she was then) made of

4

Brookfield when she came as a bride, nobody knows. My great-grandfather, Sergeant Benjamin Francis Archer, who was said to have fought at Waterloo, was the official tenant at the time and he was said to be a very dull man who talked of nothing but turnips. From the start, I believe Grandma made it plain that it was dashing Daniel William that she had married, with his black stovepipe hat set at a jaunty angle and his rakish beard, and that she didn't care much for the rest of the Archers. 'There was a bit of devilment in the chep,' she'd say, admiringly, in her distinct Borsetshire accent, and then she'd look scornfully round the tea table, as if to say: 'You're a poor lot. I got the best of you!' And my father would bend his head over his plate of stew, my mother would look tight-lipped and annoyed and we boys wouldn't know what was expected of us. After all, if *we* showed signs of devilment, we had it licked out of us!

Nowadays, the first October job at Brookfield is to put the ewes to the ram. We like to do it on the first of the month, so that the ewes will start lambing in the last week of February, and I was up at the sheep pens the other day with Jethro, our most senior worker, helping him to 'raddle' the rams.

It's an age-old technique is raddling. There's even a chap called the 'reddleman' in one of Thomas Hardy's novels. The idea is to mark the rams with raddle, which is simply a coloured powder mixed with oil, on the brisket behind their forelegs. When the ram mounts a ewe he leaves a mark on the ewe's back, which tells the shepherd that the ewe has been 'visited'. Since Hardy's time the system has been refined to enable the shepherd, by using a sequence of colours, to manage his flock more efficiently. At Brookfield, for instance, we start with yellow and use that for eight days; then we change the raddle to red and use that until the seventeenth day; then we switch to blue. Generally speaking, most of the flock

5

is marked in those first seventeen days, although some ewes won't have taken the ram at all and others will be marked twice, showing that they didn't hold to the first service. A good shepherd tries to end up with three groups by the time he takes the rams out in November and that makes for easier handling in the days before lambing.

Anyway, we like to freshen up the raddle each day and that was what Jethro was busy at with seven rams to daub, hefty beggars some of them as big as donkeys. When he had finished, we drove up on to Lakey Hill, where one or two of the ewes had been showing signs of foot rot, and I helped Jethro get them into a pen so that he could treat them. Every so often he would call out, 'That all right then, boss?' more out of sensitivity for the feelings of a retired chap like me than because he didn't know what to do, and I would call back, 'Aye, that's right, Jethro,' and he would say, 'Rightie-ho, then!' as if I'd been an invaluable help, when all I was doing was leaning against the Land-Rover, enjoying the sunshine.

There's no view in all England, to my mind, to compare with the view from Lakey Hill. In the distance there's the smudge of the Malverns, but I like to look closer to home, to the Vale of Am, with the village, the winding river and the surrounding farms. Three of them are connected to the Archer family in one way or another. Looking to the east, running up to Leaders Wood, there's Home Farm, owned by Brian Aldridge, who is married to my granddaughter Jennifer, and beyond that you can see a couple of fields of Bridge Farm, where my grandson Tony is the tenant. Then, to the south, where the land slopes up to Ten Elms Rise, there's Brookfield, and the land I've worked for most of my life.

When I first saw the light of day in the big oak-beamed front bedroom of the farmhouse, Brookfield was a 100-acre tenanted farm on the Lawson-Hope Estate. Now it stretches to more than 500 acres, my son Phil is the owner and I doubt if my father and mother would recognize the place if they came back. the house looks the same, and one or two of the older buildings have survived, but if I tell you that the yards, milking parlour, cow houses, grain stores, implement sheds, dutch barns, workshops and suchlike now cover nearly three acres (which is bigger than a football pitch) – well, you'll see why the view from the back door is very different from what it was in 1896. It's a sight different from what it was thirty years ago, when Doris and I were offered the freehold by Squire Lawson-Hope!

Like Topsy, the place has 'just growed'. Looking down from Lakey Hill, I can see ploughed fields and pastures that were once split between five or six different farms. Most fields, whether they're part of the old '100–acre' Brookfield or not, bring back memories of one sort or another.

Ashfield, for instance, used to belong to Fred Barratt, and I remember the day during the last war when Fred rang me up, almost in tears, and asked me to go over and look at his sheep – or what was left of them. Eight ewes were lying dead when I got to Ashfield and three more were so badly mauled that they had to be put down. Under a sack lay the body of one of the culprits, a big black Labrador. His mate, a terrier, had escaped Fred's second barrel.

Across the road in Marney's where Phil now has his fancy sheep-handling equipment, I once saw a threshing machine burned to a metal skeleton. That happened during the First War, when I was home on leave and had gone over to give old Joseph Marney a hand. There weren't really enough of us to cope, the chaff had begun to build up and old Joseph, who was always a bit short-tempered, set fire to a heap of it. A few minutes later the wind changed and the flames swept back towards the rick. We managed to hitch the horses to the steam engine and draw that out of the way, but we couldn't save the thresher.

7

Down in the valley, between Cow Pasture and The Croft, is the place where we calved a cow as she lay half submerged in the Am. She'd been looking for a nice sheltered spot to give birth, I daresay, and was floundering in two feet of water between the willows. Old Ned Larkin, Jethro's father, was with me, and we managed what must be one of the few underwater calvings of all time. The cow was pretty exhausted by the time we'd finished, but once she was a couple of hundredweight lighter and could see and hear her lovely roan calf, she managed to scramble out of the river none the worse for her adventure.

Beyond the farmhouse, I can see The Grove and every time I look at the ash trees by the track, I think of an afternoon back in 1920 when I was helping Josh, my father's worker, to bring in the last of the hay. As we turned out of the field, a thunderstorm broke over our heads and the first violent gust of wind brought a tree down next to the track. I think the horse heard the creaking before we did and jolted forward, saving himself and us as the huge branches came toppling down on the wagon.

Looking over to Wormitts and Lakey Meadow my mind goes back to the day the hunt found a fox in Cuckoo Covert and young Miss Smart fell badly at the hedge and broke a thigh. That was in 1936 or 1937. Walter Gabriel and a couple of other foot-followers helped me to lift a gate off its hinges and we used it as a stretcher to carry Miss Smart back to Hollowtree. On that particular morning the next field along, Burntland, was full of sows and litters in portable sties and I'll never forget how they squealed and grunted as the hunt went through them!

Five hundred and twenty acres! I can remember things that happened in every field, just about, and things that happened in fields that no longer exist, because although the land is the same, the landscape has been sadly changed, and many an old field name has gone. It's sentimental and silly, I daresay, but I can't help feeling sorry when two fields are joined together and one of the names has to go. Cow Pasture, next to the farm, used to be two fields, one of them called Stockingfield. And across the lane, what's now known as Trefoil was two enclosures, one ten acre and the other eight, and since they were joined we've lost Sunny Dingle, which ran down to Heydon Brook, and was the place where Phil and our Chris used to keep their ponies and hold gymkhanas that we all had to go and watch back in the early forties.

There's a practical reason, too, for liking the old field boundaries. They often marked out changes in soil type as well as providing useful enclosures. Our biggest field is now Badger's Bank, and that was created out of three fields with the help of a bulldozer and a government grant twenty years ago. (One of the field names we lost, by the way, was Killhorse, a very apt name for the land which slopes steeply up to Lakey Hill!) Though Badger's Bank is now one large field, when Phil comes to plant it he sometimes treats it as two, with a dividing line down the middle and a different crop on each side. The reason, of course, is that one of the hedges marked a change in soil type, and if Phil treats it all as a single field he finds it impossible to get a decent seedbed – if it's right at one end, it's still too wet at the other, or the crop ripens earlier in the old Badger's Bank than in the old Killhorse. So, you see, Nature will still have her way, even with modern farming machines and methods.

Brookfield isn't an ideal holding. For a start, we have too many fields facing north. Southern slopes are valuable because they tend to warm up more quickly and the grass and crops start growing that bit earlier, but we have a reasonable share of south-facing slopes and can't really grumble. Last March, Tony was complaining about one of his north-facing fields at Bridge Farm and young David was saying how slow it was to get the spring barley on Oakey Bank moving, and I told them: 'You

9

can't have the whole of England facing south. It would certainly be very nice but every hill has two sides you know!'

Another disadvantage caused by the way we've 'added-on' to the farm over the years, is that the house and buildings are right at one end of the place. Brookfield is nearly two miles long now and almost a mile across at its widest, and it would make things a sight easier if we could move the house and farm buildings to a site in the middle, say at the bottom of Long Field.

One thing that pleases me, though, is that we've managed to keep our farming 'balanced'. I suppose some modern business types might say we're old-fashioned because we still run a traditional 'mixed' farm with several kinds of livestock and several sorts of crops, but there's strength in diversity. Our big herd of British Friesians is the mainstay of the farm, but there's a decent herd of hybrid sows and a flock of ewes as well. We also grow wheat, barley, oilseed rape, potatoes and, of course, grass. As a young man, Phil set off at a gallop and was full of new ideas, but I'm glad he was never tempted to the extremes of specialization. My old dad had a saying which has stood at least three generations of Archers in good stead, and will probably serve David well in due course, for all his talk of computerized feeding.

> Be not the first by whom the new is tried,
> Nor yet the last to cast the old aside.

That, then, is Brookfield. A farm for all seasons, you might say, where if one crop is doing badly another is pretty sure to be doing well, and where both crops and livestock are well fitted to the land. Everything seems right and sensible, even our Jill's couple of dozen hens scratting in the farmyard.

'All is safely gathered in,' we all sang in St Stephen's on Sunday evening, 'E'er the winter storms begin.' The church was packed, as it always is for Harvest Festival, and all the farming families were there, the menfolk looking a bit uncomfortable in their cavalry-twill trousers, best jackets and brown brogue shoes. Things haven't changed much. I remember in 1919 being extremely proud of some fawn trousers and a new tweed jacket bought especially for the Harvest Festival when I had my eye on a young lass called Doris and winked at her across a row of decorative pumpkins during the sermon. She didn't dare wink back, mind. She was a lady's maid to Mrs Lawson-Hope was Doris, and had to sit with the other maids, all wearing dark-blue cloaks and straw bonnets. Next to them sat the coachman and footman wearing canary-yellow uniroms with silver buttons and, behind them, keeping a stern eye on the proceedings, sat the butler, Mr Webber, who was allowed to dress privately for church. Doris got into a terrible scrape once when she carved a rhyme under the pew front, in the place where all the maids carved rhymes during those long twice-every-Sunday Victorian services. The rhyme said:

Doris Forrest is my name,
England is my nation,
Ambridge is my dwelling place,
Lady's maid my occupation.

Apparently Mr Webber couldn't think what made Doris do such a terrible thing, and all she could say was that everybody else had done it. 'Fifty years ago, Doris!' said Mr Webber. 'Many, many things were done fifty years ago!'

We have our Harvest Festival at St Stephen's on the second Sunday in October, which is a bit later in the year than harvest celebrations in most city churches. The trouble is that the 'harvest' is a difficult thing to pin down. There are, after all, so many of them! Older country folk will still talk about the hay harvest in June,

11

when we gather in the grass for winter use (I have never, I must admit, heard anyone talk of the 'silage harvest' yet!) and at Home Farm Brian has his oilseed rape harvest in July and has drilled next year's crop by the end of August. It is true that the corn harvest is usually over in Ambridge by mid–September, but you can't really have a harvest thanksgiving then because Brian is only just thinking of lifting his beet, Phil hasn't usually started on his potatoes, and at the market garden Carol Tregorran won't start picking her Cox's for another fortnight or so.

In the end, it is a matter of compromise, and in most villages there are usually one or two farmers or their wives on the Parochial Church Council who will apply a restraining hand on the vicar who wants to celebrate too soon. In Ambridge, by the second Sunday in October, Brian can usually manage some nice washed beet to decorate the porch and Carol a bushel of apples, even if they're not Cox's. Mind you, even waiting until mid-October doesn't always get us out of trouble: I can remember one Harvest Festival back in the early sixties, before some of us had combine harvesters. It had rained off and on most of the summer, and by the time we got to August most of us thought it couldn't go on raining. But it did. We struggled on with the binder whenever it was dry and set up the sheaves in stooks, assuming that a dry spell must be round the corner, but it would have taken more than a day or two's sun to dry the lot out! The butts of the sheaves were green with all the grass and weed which had grown under the corn through the summer. And then, as the rain kept coming, the grains started sprouting in the ear, germinating and sending out shoots and roots before they'd been threshed.

The lucky farmers who managed to get their crops in found they yielded quite well, but by mid–October half the corn round Ambridge was still in the stooks and most of it never did get carted – we even had a job burning it!

The result was that at our harvest service two or three of the locals bawled out 'Some is safely gathered in – but the vicar had been warned about what was coming and smiled understandingly.

When city folk talk about the harvest they really mean the corn harvest and those waving fields of wheat and barley that used to have scarlet poppies and white corn chamomile flowers in with them, as they still do, occasionally, on the farm of Joe Grundy. Joe farms 120 acres and is a tenant of the Bellamy estate. 'I like to keep to the old ways,' he said to my grandson David, who was trying to talk to him about applying nitrogen and pesticides and goodness knows what by helicopter. Now and again I've got to agree with Joe! It may not be entirely 'cost–efficient', but there's enjoyment to be got out of a farm where wild roses grow in the hedgerows, and poppies and chamomile alongside the farmtrack.

For the dairy cows, October brings a big change. Sometime this month, usually about halfway through, they come indoors for the winter and the routine for cow and cowman takes on a completely new shape. All through the summer, day and night, the dairy herd has lived outdoors, coming in twice a day for milking and then going back to pasture. Suddenly, one day in October, they all come in for milking and don't go out again! They stay inside, day and night, until next April.

It is not a date you can enter on the calendar in advance and yet, funnily enough, it is not a date which varies much from year to year. Each season, there comes a point when you know instinctively that the time has come to bring them in. Sometimes it will be a combination of circumstances. Our Phil might notice, perhaps, that the cows are 'poaching' the pasture in Midsummer Meadow, that is to say damaging it with their hooves. At the same time David, who has done a stint in the cowshed and spent ages washing the mud off each cow's udder before he can get the clusters on, is also thinking that the time has come. Then next morning Graham Collard, the cowman, gets soaking wet fetching the cows in at six o'clock, and that will clinch it. Everyone agrees that they must come in. Even the cows are happy at the prospect. For the last few days they have been mooching around looking at the grass rather than eating it, searching for somewhere dry and out of the wind to lie. Now, for the next six months, they can live in a comfortable cubicle with self–feed silage to eat!

It is not every farmer that brings his cows in, mind you. Some herds, especially further south, are left out all year round. But they are on much lighter land; it wouldn't do on our soil, and anyway, who wants to milk outdoors in a freezing bail in the middle of January?

Then there are other herds that never go out into pasture from one year's end to the next. They have their grass cut and carted to them, a method called 'zero – grazing'. It certainly seems to work, probably because the cows are never stressed by extremes of weather, sudden frosts or excessive heat or flies, but it wouldn't do for me. Bringing the cows in is part of the farming cycle, the ebb and flow of the seasons, and, although I used to have a quiet swear now and then because of the amount of work involved, I would never want to change the system. Since it is easily the most commonly followed, it seems that most other dairy farmers agree with me.

So the cows are brought in and we move on to the next big job, lifting the potatoes. Phil is a member of a local farmers' group which owns the specialist gear – the planter and the harvester – and has a central store for the spuds when they're lifted. Most other work at Brookfield comes to a halt during the week it takes to clear our acreage and Phil sometimes wonders if potatoes are really worthwhile. There's so much *else* to be done, you see, and they don't always make much in the way of profit. Every fine autumn day spent on them is a day less for the vital job of drilling the winter wheat, and barley.

At one stage, we only drilled wheat at this time of

year, but now we try to put winter barley in as well. The plant breeders have produced barleys which give high yields and ripen about three weeks before spring–sown barley. As we've only one combine at Brookfield, and one set of chaps, anything we can do to extend the harvest period is considered a very good thing indeed. Autumn sowing has another big advantage – you don't have to worry yourself sick next February and March about the weather. You only have to look back to 1983 to see what I mean. Tens of thousands of acres meant for spring barley were never drilled at all because the ground was waterlogged.

Of course, a lot of folk will tell you that cereal growing is being overdone and they might well be right. Modern high–yielding varieties, together with sprays and fertilizers and good prices from the EEC, have caused a vast increase in corn growing. You can see it clear enough here in Ambridge. When I was a boy, most of the land was grass, with the odd field ploughed to provide feed for livestock. Now we're about fifty–fifty at Brookfield, and if you look across the valley to Home Farm, Brian Aldridge has more than 1,200 of his 1,500 acres in arable crops. We're in what they call an 'up corn, down horn' period, in other words cereals pay better than livestock. At Brookfield we've tried to keep a balance, but some folk, to my mind, have let economics and chemicals lead them the wrong way, and one of these days they'll pay for it.

There was a sharp frost during the night, and in the morning the dahlias were drooping low and curly chestnut leaves were drifting down from the trees in the Vicarage garden. Before lighting my bonfire I poked inside it carefully with a stick to make sure no hedgehogs had crawled under the dead leaves to hibernate. It had happened one year when Doris was alive and the result was very distressing for the hedgehog when the bonfire was lit. Last year one of them chose a luckier spot. I found him under some holly clippings by the back hedge and I left him as he was, being very careful not to heap more leaves on top of him than there had been to start with. Hibernation, you see, is a matter of keeping a very delicate balance. The hedgehog needs enough leaves on him to keep out the frost, but not enough to warm him up and make him breathe faster, because when that happens he uses up too much energy. Ideally, he likes to be as cold as possible without actually freezing, and when that's the case, he can get by quite comfortably, breathing once every five minutes or so.

Before the last war, the end of October brought with it a major social event in Ambridge, and that was the ploughing match. In those days there were heavy horses on every farm, and many more farms than there are now, and the annual ploughing competition was an occasion indeed. There used to be a beer tent and a tent for judging mangolds and swedes and suchlike. It all used to start at nine o'clock in the morning with about twenty teams from Edgeley, Ambridge, Penny Hassett and Waterley Cross; all with their red ribbons, tinkling bells on their heads, and polished brass ornaments on their harness.

I remember the ploughing match with such affection because it was very much a *farming* event, and one that cannot happen now. There are ploughing competitions held in several places in the country, but they're not the same as the old village match. I only need to catch a breath of crisp late–October air and I'm carried back to a morning in the mid–twenties, when I first entered a Brookfield team. I can see the ploughshares gleaming as they turned the clods of earth and the wagtails running furiously over the soil in search of their breakfasts, and I can hear the ploughmen calling 'Turn to'ard, you!' 'Come hither you!' 'Wey–a–pull–oop!' in their broad Borsetshire accents.

Each competitor had half an acre to plough; that meant a march of five miles before the job was done.

16

There was a deal of humour, mind you, with sly calls of 'bit foggy, this morning, Silas?' when Silas Winter made a furrow that was anything but straight, and much unwanted advice on the lines of 'Heads too close together, Walter, you allus needs to see a'tween your horses, lad.' There was an old farmer there, saying how ploughing matches were nothing to what they used to be and how a labourer's work was lighter than it was of old. Ploughing with an old–fashioned wooden plough, he said, was *real work*! Why, it was as much as a man could do to keep it from falling over, and, if it fell, it was beyond a boy's strength to set it right again.

It was after that particular match that Squire Lawson–Hope, giving out the prizes, criticized some of the ploughing and a carter called out from back, 'You'd best do it yourself then!' That was just what he did. 'Stand by,' he said, and ploughed a couple of furrows as straight as any man had managed that day.

It's a far cry from an old man who remembers the wooden plough to the mechanized farming we see today, but the same jobs are being done as were always done. Whatever machines you use, there's still nothing to equal the satisfaction of shutting the gate on a field after you've finished drilling it and then seeing that sheen of pale green ten days or a fortnight later. It's over sixty years since the first time I drilled my own wheat, on a small farm rented to me by the Squire just after the First War. That field was four acres and it took me nearly four days to plough it with Prince and Bessie, my two horses, using a single–furrow plough. It was a wonderful, open autumn that year. The land worked down a treat and then came the great moment when the tilth was fit for drilling. I borrowed the old drill from my dad at Brookfield, harnessed the horses to it, and persuaded Doris Forrest (I was 'walking out' with her by this time!) to lead them because Prince was playing up for some reason. It was a bit of a change from being a lady's maid at the manor, but she didn't mind and I walked behind to make sure none of the coulters got blocked.

How things have changed! Today Jethro ploughs a twenty–acre field with a sixty–horsepower diesel tractor and a three–furrow reversible plough in a couple of days, works it down with the power harrows in one pass if he's lucky. David goes up the next morning with the combine drill, putting seed and fertilizer on together and is back at Brookfield for his tea before you know it. My first field yielded eighteen hundredweight an acre when I harvested it in August 1920. Phil's field will give fifty hundredweight an acre, maybe even three ton.

It may be mechanized and scientific nowadays, but the excitement is just the same when you see a field greening up with the promise of another harvest.

NOVEMBER

I HAD just turned seven when I discovered the unpleasant side of growing up. My mother had been laid low with influenza, which was a very nasty illness in those days, and although she was on her feet again, she looked tired and washed out, even to my young and thoughtless eyes. One morning I came downstairs ready to go egg-collecting, which was my usual task, and found my father standing by the kitchen door with two buckets of pig food. 'Daniel, it's time you did more. Ben can look after the eggs.'

And that was that. Egg-collecting had been quite jolly. Now, on clammy cold mornings, I found myself struggling across the yard, my arms almost popping out of their sockets from the weight of two buckets of greasy slops. We had three pigs instead of the usual one that year, and how I hated them. How frightened I was when they came crashing into me in their greediness and made me spill their food all over my trousers and down my bare legs! I think it was my experience in those early years that made me prefer keeping sheep when I was a farmer and leave the pig side of things to Phil.

Before I had the job of egg–collecting, I had no duties at all, except sitting on the kitchen table and clapping my hands when my mother swept up beetles and threw them, wriggling, on to the fire. I think every kitchen had beetles in those days. They'd come out at night, huge invading armies of them, and scurry all over the floor, and the chairs, and the table. My mother used to put down stuff called Keatings Powder, and in the morning, the beetles would all be lying on their backs waving their legs about. I'd sit on the table and watch as she lit the fire in the grate of the 'kitchener' stove, hooking the kettle over it for the pot of tea. She would then go round sweeping up the Keatings Powder and the beetles, shooting them into the flames.

After that she'd start to get breakfast ready; and what an enormous meal it was! By the time my father and Josh came in from milking there would be porridge, thick slices of home-cured bacon would be sizzling in a frying pan, and there'd be salted pork perhaps, and huge loaves, with fresh butter, marmalade and honey. Tea would be brewed in a monster-size pot and it was nothing for my father and Josh to drink a pint mug of it each. Some farms still used to serve table beer at breakfast time, which was a weak ale made with malt but no hops, but we were considered rather an abstemious lot at Brookfield. My grandfather, Daniel William, had been a heavy drinker, but my father rarely touched alcohol at all.

It was my mother who brewed our ale, something she called 'Ruffle–me–Cap', every October and March, and it was Mother who made the butter every week and baked our bread and cakes.

Baking day was always a Friday, and once breakfast had been cleared away and my father was off back to the fields, Mother would put bundles of dry brushwood into the domed, brick–lined bread oven and keep them burning for a couple of hours until the base was covered by hot ashes. While that was happening, the dough would be rising in front of the open fire (always marked with a cross, naturally, to stop the devil from sitting on it) and my mother would be at the table making cinnamon cakes, currant buns and sugar biscuits covered in bits of candied peel. I thought it was a lovely day, Friday, when I was a little lad, and no wonder! When the oven was hot, I'd help Mother to scrape out the ashes and mop down the hot bricks with a damp cloth, then we'd stick the loaves at the back of the oven, followed by the cakes and finally the thick, sugary biscuits. After that Mother would get on with preparing the Friday dinner, which was always boiled beef for some reason, while I'd sit smelling the aroma of baking bread and waiting for the first of the biscuits to come out!

Another entire day was devoted to making butter out of our surplus cream. In my grandfather's time, indeed, it was to get cream for butter that the cows were kept in the first place. The milk itself was drunk by the family or fed back to the calves. In bad years, I believe, the family only survived because of the profit made by Grandmother's butter sales at Borchester market.

It was still a useful source of income when I was a lad. Every week, my mother salted the cream, poured it into the churn and stirred it. Moving that churn pole up and down was a weary job, Mother's back must have ached something terrible. There were times when, for no obvious reason at all, the butter would refuse to come. It's one of those things that happen on every farm now and again and, traditionally, it's always been blamed on black magic. One answer, so they said, was to put a silver spoon in with the cream because witches can't abide silver, and, if that didn't work, well, then, it meant the witch had actually *passed into* the churn. The only way to get her out, according to local wisdom, was to thrust a red hot poker in and give her a nasty shock.

I don't know if my mother tried silver spoons or pokers, but I remember Ben got a nasty shock one day when the kitchen fire had gone out because of a soot fall. There was no dinner ready and Mother was still in the dairy trying to make the butter. My father came in cold and hungry and Ben started howling to be taken to Borchester Fair. The hiding he got on his backside must have warmed him almost as much as a red–hot poker would have done!

On the first Saturday in November, the opening meet of the South Borsetshire Hunt takes place, by tradition, at

The Bull in Ambridge. There are usually fifty or sixty mounted and twice that many foot–followers, most of whom know a darned sight more about hunting than those on horses. Hunting runs through country life like the wick through a candle, although many people who ride to hounds are more interested in a good gallop and a gossip than in what has happened to the fox. Nobody enjoys a day out with the hounds more than our Shula, all togged up in her black coat and shiny boots, but ask her for an account of the day's sport and it's likely to be a very hazy affair. She was probably talking to her friend Nigel Pargetter about his holiday in Greece when the fox crossed the ride just in front of them! But Tom Forrest, who has never put on a hunting coat in his life, will not have missed much from his vantage point. He'll have seen old Charlie cross the Am and slip back up into Littleton Covert.

I was passionately keen on hunting when I was a lad, and it got me into trouble more than once. I could not *resist* a day with the hounds, you see, any more than I could resist those thick bars of nut chocolate with raisins that cost a penny each in the village shop. On one occasion – I must have been eleven or twelve I suppose – I got into even worse trouble than usual.

It was a lovely November morning with the mist still lying on the fields, and the sun coming up over Blossom Hill. The hounds were meeting at Ambridge Hall and my dad had gone off early on his pony and trap to look at a bull calf the other side of Borbury. He was not expected back until milking time. I was all ready, just like Shakespeare's reluctant schoolboy, to crawl unwillingly to school when I saw an older boy, the son of a weathly farmer down at Traitor's Ford, hacking along the lane towards the meet.

That was it! I played truant. I was heedless of what my dad would do when he found out (somebody was sure to see me and tell him) or of the solemn, sorrowful face of our vicar's wife, a pretty girl of about twenty–five who talked to us about honesty and proper obedience and suchlike in Sunday school. I was going hunting for the day!

The hounds found in Foxholes, a covert which now forms part of Brookfield Farm, and the fox set his mask for Ten Elms Rise. I was on my little black pony, Pitch, who was not even shod. He must have stood all of eleven hands high, but I dug my heels into him and he flew. Hounds went at a cracking pace and all went well until we got into a field near Pettifer's Barn with a big thorn hedge at the far end. All around horses thundered towards it, and me and Pitch thundered along with them. The closer that hedge came the bigger it seemed to get, but ahead of us, horses were sailing over it . . .

I don't know if you are familiar with an old poem called 'The Risks of the Game', but it might well have been written about me and Pitch:

> The dark–brown steed on the left was there,
>   On the right was a dappled grey,
> And between the pair, on a chestnut mare,
>   The duffer who writes this lay.
> What business had 'this child' there to ride?
>   But little or none at all;
> Yet I held my own for a while 'in the pride
>   That goeth before a fall'.

Well, I had the pride all right, but Pitch had the common sense. He decided against the hedge and I sailed over it all by myself, landing in about three feet of muddy water on the other side. When my head stopped spinning round all I could see was Mr Lovell, who used to farm Troutbridge, sitting there on his horse roaring with laughter. Then he got off and helped me up. Pitch was grazing quietly on the other side of the hedge. I insisted on remounting him and following the hunt for a bit, but they lost the fox in the wood and I went home.

I got ticked off by my mother for getting wet, walloped

by my father for taking the pony, caned the next day at school for playing truant and, on Sunday, the vicar's pretty young wife looked at me with big sad eyes and said, 'Oh Daniel' in a way that made me feel terrible. But it was worth it!

Hounds do not get the runs they used to nowadays, mainly because of changes in agricultural practice. For one thing, as I was saying earlier, there is far more arable land these days: up until the Second World War most of the land in these parts was in grass, with just the odd field down to corn to provide feed. Until myxomatosis came in the fifties and killed most of the rabbits, nobody worried about horses treading the headlands of the cornfields, because the rabbits would have had most of the young corn anyway. (I can remember growing wheat in pre-myxomatosis days and going round one field twice with the binder before we had enough sheaves for a single stook.)

Nowadays, though, with land costing £2,000 an acre, and rents often up in the £50–to £60–an–acre range, and the enormous cost of growing high–yielding crops, farmers are far from keen to see the hunt cantering across their winter barley, even if the Hunt Secretary assures them that they won't know where the horses have been by the end of the winter! There aren't even the stubbles to gallop over these days; no sooner are the straw bales cleared than the cultivation equipment moves in and, before cubbing's over, they are back in oilseed rape or winter corn.

Most farmers enjoy hunting, especially over somebody else's land! But they dislike it on their own, and it is my guess that it will not be the 'antis' who put a stop to hunting, but farming itself. Still, it won't happen for a long time, and the opening meet of the South Borsetshire Hunt is still at The Bull, Ambridge, just like it always was, and Sid Perks, the landlord, has a worried look on his face as he wanders round with his tray of drinks, making sure all the mounted followers get a

24

glass, but also that he does not miss out one of his regulars. I hope he sees me!

Joe Grundy, who was the earth–stopper for the hunt for many years, was in The Bull the other night arranging to sell some apples to Mr Fletcher who's bought one of the new houses at Glebelands. 'Real *country* apples, you don't mind a few wasp bites in them I hope?' he asked. Mr Fletcher said of course he didn't. He bought Joe another pint, and one for me as well, and said how much he enjoyed talking to a couple of old countrymen. Joe was in a mellow mood (not surprising, having sold two boxes of bruised windfalls) and recited what he said was an old Borset rhyme about the weather, 'If the sun's still riding high, your crops are sure to die.' Then he said: 'Soon be the killing time, of course.'

'Will it?' asked Mr Fletcher.

'Kill your pig and bung your barrel,' said Joe. 'That's right, ain't it, Dan?'

I had to agree that St Martin's Day, 11 November, was the traditional day for villagers to kill the backyard pig they had been fattening up all summer. It was also the date when cider making ought to be over and done with.

Nowadays there are few farmers who bother to make their own cider. It is a lot easier to send your apples off to a factory and get a few barrels back in due course, and you have to look a long way to find a villager who keeps a pig in his back garden. Susan Carter, who lived in one of the council houses on the Green before she got married, tried it and ended up in terrible trouble. First somebody from Glebelands complained about the pig getting loose, then she was visited by a hygiene inspector, then an official came and said that cats, dogs and budgies were the only pets allowed on council property. In the end Susan had to sell her pig to Eddie Grundy.

Up until the end of the war, though, there were, 'pig-clubs' in every village, groups of men who bought pigfood wholesale and usually arranged a contract with a butcher to kill their pigs in due course. Although Martinmas was the traditional killing time (a tradition that goes right back to the Middle Ages, when everything except the breeding stock had to be slaughtered and salted), cottagers' pigs could be killed any time from October to December.

And what an event it was, when I was a boy! We had a few pigs at Brookfield, of course, but it was the annual killing of the Gabriel family pig that I remember most vividly.

Walter Gabriel's dad was more fond of his pig than anything, including Walter, and he housed it in a very luxurious sty at the bottom of their garden in Back Lane. He grew his own barley and parsnips to feed it on, because he reckoned imported maize made the pig's blood run hot and made the bacon turn yellow on the rack. He would only kill the animal when the moon was on the wane. When the big day came, he would send for the pig sticker, who would arrive wearing his blue smock and blue-and-white striped apron. Walter and me and Walter's little sister Alice would go out to watch. Walter's dad always looked a bit miserable when the pig was being stuck (so expertly, mind you, that it never felt a thing), but then he had been going down the garden to scratch the creature's back every evening for the past three or four months.

The following day the pig sticker would come back to cut up the pig, but Walter's mum would already have been at work in the kitchen. It still amazes me to think what a countrywoman could make out of one average-sized pig fifty years ago. There would be sausages and pork pies, the head would be boiled down to make pork cheese (or brawn), there would be chitterlings (beautiful, eaten all hot and greasy by a small boy on a cold winter's day) and the best faggots anyone has ever tasted. The 'leaf' from a fat bacon pig would give twenty pounds of lard and, when the fat was drained, there

26

would be lovely, crisp, golden scratchings left. There would be pig's pudding made out of the blood, and saveloys – most of this was made out of the 'left-overs' – because the joints and sides were turned into hams and bacon to feed the family through the winter.

Each family in the village had its own recipe for making bacon, and I know that when Doris salted a pig at Brookfield she used to put brown sugar and juniper berries in with the brine before packing the joints into the salting lead. Before the last war a traveller used to visit Ambridge twice a year selling wedge-shaped bars of Droitwich salt especially for the purpose. The main joints would be packed into the lead and then, if not used for other purposes, the pig's feet, the cheek, and the jowls. (That, by the way, is where the phrase 'cheek by jowl' comes from!)

Joe Grundy at Grange Farm is about the only chap left round Ambridge who salts his own bacon and he is the only farmer left who makes his own cider. Ambridge is not a fruit-growing county, although most farms have an old orchard out at the back. At Brookfield the trees are mainly Blenheims, Prince's Pippins, and a few northern greens. There are also three trees that nobody can identify. I bought them for 2s.6d. each in the market in 1956, and the chap who was selling them said they came from Holland.

In the thirties there was a cider press at Wynyards Farm that served most of the area, and late every October me and Doris, with young Jack helping us, would collect the apples at Brookfield into heaps, (apart from a basket or two of Blenheims for the house) and leave them until the pressure of ploughing and drilling the corn was over. By early November, those apples would be in a fine old state, what with the hens and geese pecking at them, the calves snuffling round them and butterflies and bees feasting themselves, but it didn't seem to matter. When we had the time we would heave them into a wagon, and take them round to the cider press at Wynyards.

27

You can often remember things best by smell, and even today, if I pass Grange Farm when Joe's cider-making and smell the fermenting fruit, it takes me staight back to that old press in the stone barn at Wynyards, and I can see the hurricane lamps shining on the packed cheeses of apple pulp and straw, and two old chaps turning the handle while the cider juice is squeezed slowly out. Wireless was spreading through the country at that time and it was such a craze that folk were rigging them up everywhere. The two chaps at Wynyards had one in the barn and they often made cider until late at night to the sound of a tango band playing in one of London's smartest hotels. At the end of the evening, the man on the wireless would say 'Goodnight, everybody, goodnight,' and they would stop what they were doing and shout 'Goodnight!' back to him.

We were sitting round the fire at Brookfield the other night and David, who had just got back from a Young Farmers' meeting, was telling us how we would have to alter our calving pattern when there was a knock at the door. It was Graham Collard, the cowman, 'I think we're going to have to give Priscilla a hand,' he said. 'You know, number ninety-eight, the one we had trouble with the last time round.' Graham is not the sort of chap to panic, so without asking any questions Phil and David slipped on their leggings and gum-boots, donned their working coats and set off across the yard.

Since we *haven't* yet altered our calving pattern, we still try to calve in autumn, which, in effect, means that we have something like a hundred cows calving between September and December. That is roughly one a day, but it does not happen as conveniently as that! We are more likely to go three days without one and have four calves in a day (usually at the weekend according to Graham). So a tap on the door at ten o'clock at night is not unusual. Few cowmen are happy going to bed leaving potential trouble and it is usually better to sort a cow out late at night than risk coming down to a dead calf in the morning.

There are really three sorts of calving. The best is when the cow goes off and does it on her own and the first thing you know about it is when you go to get the cows in and there she is on the other side of the field licking her newly born calf. In the winter, you may have noticed the early signs of calving and put her in a separate box, then when you poke your head over the door an hour later, you find it is over and done with. The second sort is when the cow needs some help, but it is a straightforward job and you don't need to call in the vet. It may mean searching around for that missing forefoot or straightening the head and that sort of thing, but you can sense that there are no complications. The third type of calving is when you know from experience that the job is beyond you. It may be something as simple as a big calf with just not enough room, or may be a malpresentation, or even twins, but I would always bring in the vet rather than risk cow or calf. His £20 bill is a fleabite compared to the £120 the calf represents, or the £600-odd which it would cost to replace the mother. In practice, we call out the vet surprisingly rarely, but I never begrudged the fee involved, even if I sometimes felt afterwards that I could have managed on my own.

Having said all that, there were times when I tried to manage on my own, and nearly came unstuck. Years and years ago I went out to a cow, Lupin her name was. She'd been messing around trying to calve ever since dinnertime, and it must have been about two o'clock in the morning when I left my warm bed to make sure everything was all right. The wind was whipping round the yard, rattling the corrugated iron and I nearly got blown along to the cowshed. Lupin gave a little grunt when she saw me in the light from the hurricane lamp, and well she might because she was in a lot of trouble. The calf was half out – more than half – but seemed to be firmly stuck at the hips. The poor creature had obviously

29

been straining for some time, and the calf's eyes were starting out of its head and its tongue was sticking out. I didn't know what to do. I doubted if I had enough strength to pull the calf out (I learned later that it was the last thing to try to do anyway), but Lupin obviously couldn't cope on her own. Just as I was wondering whether to go for the vet, I heard a rustle of straw and Doris came up behind me. She'd woken up, found my side of the bed empty, and guessed that there was trouble of some kind. It was Doris, bless her, who remembered what the vet had done the last time we had this sort of problem. Instead of tugging he had simply *lifted* the little creature out, over its mother's pelvis. So that was what we tried and it slipped quietly out, a heifer, red all over just like its mother. 'Now I'll go and make a cup of tea,' said Doris, who was a grand farmer's wife!

Anyway, the other night Jill offered to run me home, but I've been a farmer too long to want to go without finding out what was happening across the cowshed. So, after 'wrapping up warmly' as Jill put it, I was allowed to wander over and arrived just at the right moment. It was a straightforward job, fortunately. Graham and David each had a cord attached to one of the calf's forelegs and Phil was standing behind the cow, gently easing the head through the vulva. Both David and Graham were a study in strength and gentleness. 'She would probably have been all right,' said Phil, 'but it's better to be on the safe side.' Five minutes later the calf lay steaming on the floor of the box, the cow busy licking it clean. The others went to wash themselves, but I waited, leaning over the half door of the box for another ten minutes until the magic moment when the little creature struggled to its feet and began edging its way, instinctively, towards the cow's udder and its first suck of warm milk.

Remembrance Sunday. In church this morning Colonel Danby laid a wreath on the stone memorial in the nave.

It is a job I had myself for many years, when I was chairman of the parish council. I daresay the colonel was thinking of 1939-45, when he served as an officer in Burma, but twelve of the fourteen names on the memorial belong to men who fell in the First War.

In The Bull, afterwards, Sid had a good fire lit in the Ploughman's and I had a pint while I waited for Shula to collect me and take me up to Brookfield for lunch. When Joe came in, Mr Fletcher tried to complain to him about his boxes of apples. 'I know you said there'd be a few wasp bites, old chap, but dash it all . . . .'

'I don't think,' said Joe, who was wearing his suit and a collar and tie, 'I can talk about apples. Not today, if you don't mind.'

Mr Fletcher looked bewildered and bought him a drink. Joe told him about his Uncle Ted. 'Called up in the Derby scheme and served under Major General Dundersville,' he said in his ponderous voice, making it sound as if his uncle had been a horse. 'All the way from Mesopotamia to Persia with the Dirty Warwicks.'

Mr Fletcher asked about Joe's own military experience, and Joe muttered something about having been too young for the first and too old for the second, which was less than strictly accurate as he was born in 1921. 'We had a tough enough time fighting the Ministry of Agriculture,' he added.

In the Second World War, I was chairman of one of the local agricultural committees and I can remember the occasional tussle with Joe and his dad, trying to make them grow the crops the Ministry in London said we all *ought* to be growing, and plough up land they didn't want to plough. What I remember most, however, was the way natural food surpluses suddenly affected the diet of the whole country. In a good season for turnips, the Ministry for Food shoved out hundreds of turnip recipes, in a tomato glut they urged us all to eat tomatoes. Many people thought it was the Ministry bungling the national growing programme by constantly giving us too much of

31

one food and not enough of another, but farming has always been a matter of swings and roundabouts, bad weather conditions for one crop generally favouring something else.

How those Ministry chaps worked at making folk eat what they didn't want to eat! In the autumn of 1940 it was potatoes, and I came across a leaflet about it, stuck inside one of my old record books, only the other day. This is what it said:

P's for Protection Potatoes afford,
O's for the Ounces of energy stored.
T's for Tasty and vitamins rich in,
A's for the Art to be learned in the kitchen.
T's for Transport, we need not demand,
O's for Old England's own food from the land.
E's for Energy eaten by you,
S's for the spuds that will carry us through!

The leaflet also had a recipe on it for coffee potato scones, which were really ordinary potato cakes but with half a cup of strong sweetened coffee added. I have no idea what they tasted like, although Doris had put a tick against the recipe, so we must have tried it. 'Food is a munition of war,' said the leaflet, finally. 'Now, here's your part in the fight for victory! When a particular food is not available, cheerfully accept something else. Keep loyally to the rationing regulations!'

I was over forty when the Second World War broke out, but I was of a very suitable age to be a fighting soldier in the First War. I was conscripted in 1916, but before then I had worked for several months as a carter's lad in the hay trade and that, surprisingly enough, influenced my entire army career! When the war started both the carters working for Mr Blower, the Hollerton hay merchant, were called up. They were reservists, you see, and he had a difficult time replacing them. As a result I was taken on during the winter of 1915, as soon

32

as ploughing and drilling were finished at Brookfield, on the basis of 2s. 6d. a day 'journey money' to drive a load of hay from Ambridge into Borchester. I used to pick the load up outside The Bull at four o'clock in the morning. The pub used to be open serving beer like nobody's business. Most pubs were open all day and most of the night, and it wasn't until nearly the end of the war that DORA (the Defence of the Realm Act) brought in such things as licensing laws.

Anyway, when I was called up I didn't find myself in France or Palestine, but in a camp near Darrington helping to procure hay for the army. And quite a job it was! Before the First War, hay had been fetching perhaps £5 a ton, but it rocketed to £16 in no time, and farmers were still unwilling to sell it. Our job was to make sure they sold it to the army, at the proper price, whether they liked it or not. There was me, four other lads and a certain Sergeant Rutter, a man who told us that his family were famous poachers who had been persecuted by farmers since time immemorial. Now, of course, the boot was on the other foot. We would go along to a farm somewhere and have a glass of beer in the kitchen while the farmer told us how poor the hay harvest had been and how he was going to have to sell off his livestock at this rate. Sergeant Rutter would nod in a sympathetic way, and we'd have a drop more beer and perhaps a bite of beef and pickles, then we'd go outside. There the farmer would show us his hay, making a great point of the number of animals he had to feed. He would tell us how he would spare some hay if he could but really he couldn't. That was when Sergeant Rutter remembering all the farmers who had hounded 'they Rutters' would point to a haystack and say: 'His Majesty will have that!'

However much the farmer complained we would go and shove a long iron into the stack, a funny implement that opened up into a sort of umbrella inside so the farmer could not pull it out, and had a plate on the end with W.D. on it.

Some farmers got up to the most amazing tricks, storing hay in their bedrooms and lofts. One cunning old chap covered a complete haystack with straw after he had finished threshing his wheat one back end. We would never have known if a sudden breeze hadn't blown a bit off just at the wrong moment.

It sounds a peculiar way to have fought a war, I know, but hay was the oil and petrol of the British army in 1914-18, and because the French could not supply enough for their own beasts most of it had to be sent across the Channel after being 'compressed' by a special machine. In May 1917 I was on the point of being posted to Dover to a receiving station set up to take in horses returned as 'unusable' from France and known as 'army –casts', but my father became seriously ill, and through the intervention of Colonel Lawson–Hope I was sent home to look after the farm.

Things ought not to happen that way, I know, but when the Colonel went to war he had taken half the village men marching with him and once in the war he tried to look after them. It was all part of a world that was destroyed at Passchendale and can never return. I was one of the lucky ones.

One crop I never really got on with was sugar beet. We don't grow it at Brookfield, but I did have a go a time or two in the thirties and again in the sixties. Perhaps we were just unlucky with the weather, but it seemed an awful lot of hard work for very little return. Mind you, that was in the days before they got the crop fully mechanized. We had to spend hours hoeing the blessed things in May and June, followed by several weeks' hard labour in November ploughing them out, then a lot of effort knocking the mud off, cutting the tops off and loading the beet into a horse-drawn cart.

That was when I tried it in the thirties. The other day I was watching Brian Aldridge harvesting his beet. He had already topped them by machine and put the tops to one

34

side for the sheep to eat. Now he was busy with a huge three–row lifter which was shooting the beet out into a trailer travelling alongside. I was only there an hour but he must have lifted an acre in that time, work that would have taken us a couple of days by hand.

I think Phil's right, though: our land is too heavy for sugar beet except in a really good year and who can forecast one of those? But it's a fascinating crop, and it's developed in Britain almost entirely in my lifetime. The first sugar beet factory is said to have been opened in 1832 by Quakers who disapproved of the slave trade which helped to produce cane sugar, but the crop was never grown on any scale until the twenties. These days about half our sugar comes from cane, imported from tropical countries, and the other half comes off our own land. The beet from Brian's 100 acres alone produces nearly 250 tons of actual sugar.

Although it is still a tricky and not particularly profitable crop to grow, modern techniques have taken nearly all the backache out of it. The seed is sown in the spring but preparations start in the autumn, when Brian puts farmyard manure from his beef cattle onto the stubble of the previous cereal crop, and ploughs it in so that the frost can get to work on the upturned soil during the winter. What he is hoping for is a good seedbed in March. At the latest he wants to get his beet drilled before the middle of April, after which every week's delay probably means a ton an acre less of beet.

He uses what is called a precision drill, which deposits one seed about every seven inches, and sprays it with a pre-emergence weedkiller. Apart from perhaps one more spray and one pass with a tractor hoe, that should be that until the autumn, unless there is an attack of aphids in June, in which case he may have to spray to kill them because they spread the dreaded virus yellow disease.

They're a keen lot, sugar-beet growers, always eyeing each other's crops over the hedge to see if they are doing better than their own. They like to see the leaves meeting across the rows by the end of June. This stops the land drying out and also exposes plenty of leaf to the sun – the more leaf there is to catch the sun the more sugar will be stored in the roots, and they base the price of the crop on the sugar percentage.

Sugar beet will go on growing quite happily until November, when the frosts come. Brian is in no hurry to start harvesting them because he has plenty of other work on during October and he knows his beet are putting on weight and increasing in value day by day, but he never knows what the weather is going to be like. So, in practice, he tends to start about the third week of October and hopes to finish in a month. Normally, he has them all out of the ground well before the Smithfield Show at the beginning of December, but there was one year, not so long ago, when he was harvesting them until nearly Christmas.

The beet, long white roots like overgrown parsnips, are dumped on a concrete pad and then the fun with the factory permit starts. The beet factories are only open for about four months each year, during which time they have to deal with the best beet from nearly half a million acres. Once the crop is lifted every farmer wants to get it to the factory before it gets frosted or loses weight or sugar. So the factory issues permits; so many lorry loads a week, based on the size of the crop. A few years back one cheeky grower from Borbury got a permit for so many fifteen–ton lorry loads, then booked Fred Baker's twenty-ton truck and carted in the same number of loads. The factory soon found out what was going on, but, in the meantime, he had got rid of quite a few extra tons!

In some ways, I wish we did grow beet at Brookfield. I know our milk ends up as pintas on the doorstep, and some of our wheat finds its way into your bread and, of course, we produce quite a few rashers of bacon during the year, but none of these has the mystery or the magic between farm and breakfast table as the conversion of those muddy roots into the sugar we stir into our tea.

36

DECEMBER

I WAS in The Bull, and Joe Grundy had just bought me a half of best bitter 'with the compliments of the season', when Mr Fletcher came in with a very worried look on his face.

'Joe,' he said, 'I want a word about those logs. I think there must have been some mistake.'

'Oh?' said Joe, eyeing him over his cider mug. 'Ain't Eddie brought them round yet then?'

'Oh he's brought them,' said Mr Fletcher, 'but there don't seem to be very many, if you see what I mean. Not for £30.'

'You got a load,' said Joe. '£30 a load. That was the price agreed. We shook hands and you gave me the money right here in this bar.'

'I know I did,' said Mr Fletcher, in a regretful voice, 'but we didn't precisely specify how big a load was.'

'Well it's a load, isn't it?' said Joe. 'A load's a load, stands to reason.'

'It looks more like a very small pile to me . . .'

'It's the same load as we always give,' said Joe, getting excited, 'and those were apple logs. Sweet-smelling apple logs. You wouldn't get apple logs from a Borchester dealer. Spitting willow, that's what you'd have got, and burned holes in your Axminster else the whole house burned down!'

It ended up with Mr Fletcher buying Joe a pint and getting one in for Eddie. But he still didn't look very cheerful. 'That holly might have been a special variety,' he said, 'but it hasn't got many berries on it, not for £5.'

'Don't,' said Joe, 'talk to me about holly.'

Then he told us about what he called the 'great holly swindle' that happened a few years ago, when a scruffy-looking chap in a battered pick-up had driven into his yard and offered to 'take the holly off your hands, guv'nor'. The chap suggested a fiver, and Joe talked him up to a tenner, and for several days while Joe and Eddie were busy clearing culverts and digging drains (so Joe said) they watched the pick-up driving in and out with loads of beautifully berried holly roped to the back. It was only later, reading the *Borchester Echo*, that Joe discovered that holly was fetching £20 a hundredweight at the holly sales in Tenbury.

'I was cheated,' said Joe. 'Done rotten by that thieving, lying townie. It happens to us countrymen all the time,' he went on, glaring over his mug at Mr Fletcher.

'Yes but about *my* holly . . .' Mr Fletcher said.

'And that wasn't the end of it,' Joe said, and told us how the man in the pick–up came the next year, again offering to help Joe with his holly, and Joe sent him packing with a few well–chosen words, only to wake up the next morning and find all the holly bushes stripped. 'Gone in the night!' said Joe. 'Not a berry left!'

Mr Fletcher beat a hasty retreat, and I drank up and went back to Glebe Cottage for my dinner. Afterwards I sat down for a doze, as I do most afternoons these days. There was Brookfield holly on my mantelpiece, and apple logs burning in my hearth, because like Joe I find them easy–burning and sweet-smelling. I always keep a special supply, well dried out, for burning at Christmas.

Ash logs, they always reckoned, are the best to burn and sycamore is always very good. Oak needs to be stored for several years and then split. Willow has the devil in it, and spits and flares. It was a great favourite with me when, as a boy, I used to sit in front of the kitchen fire at Brookfield in the evenings.

'There goes the parson, there goes the clerk,' my mother would recite as the sparks flew up the chimney, or, as they shot out onto the stone-flagged floor: 'There go the people out in the dark.' She told us too about the old belief in the 'coming stranger': that if you looked into the flickering fire you would see the face of the next unknown person to visit the house. She told us how the village girls looked in the fire to see the face or form of the man they would marry. (Mind you, they used to look for that in all sorts of places, from the church porch at midnight on Midsummer's eve to a reflection in their bedroom mirror after they had brushed their hair a certain number of times.)

Throughout the twelve days of Christmas the parlour at Brookfield would be decorated with holly and mistletoe, but it was in the big kitchen, on Christmas Eve, that the official 'farm celebration' took place. At dinnertime my dad would come in with old Josh and whoever else was working for us at the time, and Mum would serve up beef and plum pudding, and Dad and the two men would drink a fair amount of beer, and Mum would say, with mock severity, 'Well, there'll be no more work done on this farm today, that I can see!'

It was a very *uproarious* sort of dinner – just a lot of food and drink, and old Josh's face getting redder, and my dad smoking his pipe and throwing out the odd remark like, 'Threshin' engine'll be'ere fortnight Monday then.' Once Ben was getting very restive – we knew all about the singing and jollity that took place on the bigger farms you see – and demanded that old Josh play us a tune on his fiddle. 'Fiddle?' said old Josh, indignantly, 'what fiddle? I can't play no fiddle.'

In the weeks leading up to Christmas we had fattened up the cockerels and taken them to market, and like Joe Grundy (though more successfully!) we had harvested our holly and our mistletoe. In those days it was quite big business on the smaller farms round Ambridge. It didn't bring in a great deal of money, but it grew for nothing. It was a time well spent to cut holly from the field hedges and mistletoe that sprouted in great berried bunches from the apple trees near the farmhouse. Many a time I

39

was despatched with a cartload of the stuff to Borchester Market, after protesting that there was no room for me to sit. 'Plenty of room up there, boy,' I'd be told as I was lifted up and perched on the front, the reins thrust into my hand and the holly pricking my backside all the way to Borchester.

The price we got used to depend very much on supply and demand, but generally speaking the more berries the more it fetched, and we had a lovely variegated tree at Brookfield which always sold well. Alas, it was rooted out in one of the many field enlargements which have taken place in recent years, and selling holly doesn't come terribly high on the list of farming priorities at Brookfield these days.

In the week before Christmas, the Squire used to send his head keeper round the village with a brace of pheasants for each farmer and a couple of rabbits for each cottager. I can't say if the Squire really thought game was such a rarity on a labourer's table, but I'm sure the keepers knew the amount of poaching that went on. There was hardly a worker in the village who didn't grab at a rabbit or pheasant if he got the chance. 'A rabbit', folk used to say, 'is nobbut eightpence running round on four legs.' But there was none of the organized poaching you get nowadays and nobody to my recollection ever touched the deer in the park.

To my dad both rabbits and pheasants were the most terrible nuisance. He could just about stand rabbits eating the corn, because rabbits were part of nature, but it drove him wild when young pheasants came swooping out of the woods and into his crop. The pheasant is a forager like anything else and, although the keepers were supposed to feed them each day, they still wandered out into the fields. One year, when they were particularly troublesome, my dad had a blazing row with the head keeper (keepers were a very arrogant breed of men, strutting round in duck egg-green suits and poaching more game than anybody according to popular

40

belief). The head keeper complained to the Squire. My dad stood up for himself, though, and even got his rent reduced, but it was no satisfaction, whatever the rent, to grow corn and see daft birds eating it up.

At least, we could get our own back on the rabbits, and there were few things in my childhood as exciting as going out to net them on a dark winter's night. I must have been eight or nine the first time I was allowed to go along. My mother thought I was tucked up safe in bed, but my dad gave a low whistle and I slipped down the back stairs and out into the yard, where he was waiting with Ned, one of our workers, and Gyp our dog. We went to a field by the road. It was a perfect night for what we were about, pitch dark and with a near–gale blowing down towards us out of the woods. The rabbits, we reckoned, would have come out of the trees at dusk and nibbled their way well into the pasture by now. As quietly as he could, my dad hammered a row of hazel sticks into the ground, their white, whittled tops glimmering faintly in the blackness, and then strung the net (which was so light that an eighty-yard length of it could fit into a coat pocket) along them. Then Ned took Gyp and disappeared along the hedge, round the field, to the edge of the wood. I crouched down, one hand on the end of the net, the wind howling down through the oak trees and almost blowing me over. After a few minutes (although it seemed like a deal longer), Ned must have released Gyp because the net jerked and my dad was darting past me, pulling a rabbit from the net, breaking its neck and throwing it clear. Then there was another thud, and another, as the rabbits came fleeing from the blackness towards us. My dad was cursing for fear the net would be torn. . . .

We caught thirty rabbits that night, and carried them home strung on poles, their legs threaded together. Fat rabbits they were too that fetched a good price at Borchester market – and so they should have, having fed on the Brookfield crops right through the summer and autumn!

* * *

Nowadays, December is what you might call a 'quietly busy' month on a farm like Brookfield. There is nothing to harvest, and not much drilling is done except when the early part of the month is very dry and mild. Corn drilled at this time of year generally takes longer to germinate and can fall prey to too many pests to make it a popular sowing time, even if you do increase the seed rate.

But, with plenty of livestock, you are never short of a job. After you have coped with the milking, feeding, mucking out and bedding of over 100 dairy cows and about 80 young stock from day-old calves to down-calving heifers, have hauled out silage to 300 ewes and checked them over, have seen to 60 sows and perhaps 500 other pigs from those just farrowed to those about to go off to market, there isn't much time left! Especially when hardly a day goes by without a minor crisis of one sort or another, from a tricky farrowing to a scouring calf, or a cow with milk fever, or perhaps a phone call to say that your sheep are in a neighbour's corn.

It surprises me, still, the way other jobs manage to get done. I was up at Brookfield last week, looking for a bit of timber to patch up my old garden shed. The yard and workshop were completely deserted. Eventually, I found Graham replacing the teat cup liners in the dairy and asked him where in Heaven's name everybody was. Phil, he told me, was across in Lakey Meadow, having a go at the moles (he won't trust anyone else with strychnine and I don't blame him); David was ploughing the Willow Bed; Neil was cutting up the big apple tree that came down in the storm last month; and Jethro was laying the hedge along the roadside by Five Acre ('It'll look lovely as folks drive along there, Master Phil,' I could just hear him saying!).

Although there are always jobs to be done there is also less pressure than at other times, and now that farm workers get four weeks' annual holiday – they deserve it, too, I might add – farmers try to persuade them to take some of it during the quiet mid–winter months. It is quite usual for one or two of the men to be off from Christmas Eve until the New Year, which probably accounts for the 'tradition' that poor Phil is always the one who has to get up at six o'clock and do the milking on Christmas morning!

Another tradition in the family is that, although I might occasionally miss the Royal Show or Smithfield, I never miss the Christmas Fatstock Show in Borchester. It is true, I've been going for almost as long as I can remember, since before the First War at any rate. My dad never entered anything, because it was the chaps breeding herds of beef cattle who entered in those days, but he always liked to go along, to look at the entries and watch them being auctioned off. He took me with him the year I left school, and sounded quite proud as he introduced me to folk as 'My eldest lad, Daniel'. At dinnertime, we went into one of the market pubs and had a 'cut off the joint' followed by rice pudding, and a pint of mild to wash it down with. No wonder the Fatstock Show has had an air of excitement and romance about it ever since!

If I was pleased with myself I was also thoroughly jealous of a schoolmate, Silas Winter. He had got a job as stockman's assistant with Mr Hickman, who had the Herefords near Loxley Barratt. The Borchester Show was 'piddlin' small beer' he said, because he was off to enter a couple of beasts in the Birmingham Fatstock Show. And he did! He was away from home four or five days, which seemed a most extraordinary thing and, when he came back, you'd think he had been herding yaks in Tibet or hunting lions in Africa the way he went on about his experiences. For weeks, he couldn't open his mouth without saying, 'Yes but when I was in Birmingham. . . ' He did have an interesting story to tell, mind you. The folk in Birmingham, apparently, were all devils, and he and another stockman had to sleep in the stall alongside their cattle every night to stop some villain coming along and interfering with their beasts. A usual trick, he said, was to give cows an extra feed, which made them scour and spoiled their chances during the judging. He had also heard of ruthless breeders who forced their beasts to wear lead jackets for two months before the show, to press their flesh into exactly the right shape for the judges. Others, he claimed, injected tallow under the skin of their animals to get the same result.

I don't think you get that sort of faking and trickery nowadays, but keen farmers know all sorts of ways to get their entries into perfect condition. A couple of years ago I was invited to see some cattle near Edgeley by an old chap who has had the Borchester Fatstock Cup on his sideboard a good few times over the years. He took me round the back of the buildings to a couple of loose boxes that were well away from the noise of any other farm activity – and that, he said, was secret number one. Don't let your beasts have any distraction. The second tip was to keep them in a building without a stable door, and when we got inside, I found that a small amount of light was coming into the buildings from ground level. 'If he wants to look at the light he has to keep his head down,' I was told, 'and that stops him getting slack backed. Can't win the cup if they're all belly and no back.' Another tip was about feeding. I can't remember the details but I know beans came into it. 'Not too many, mind, 'I was warned, 'or that'll make his blood hot.'

The old chap obviously realized that my days of entering beasts for the show were over, but he was there himself, that December, leading his entry round the judging ring and collecting a second prize. He gave me a crafty grin as he saw me watching.

The Borchester Show is only a one–day affair, and it's usually held on the Tuesday after Smithfield. Being close to Christmas there is a festive air about the place, and the auctioneers always provide a tot of whisky and a cigar for everyone after the champion has been sold. 'It cost us a fair bit, I can tell you,' one of them complained to a group of farmers one day. 'You get it back off us the rest of the year!' came the swift reply.

The show judges are usually a couple of butchers and you can see, by looking at the champion beasts, which breeds and crosses are producing the sort of beef the public wants. Tastes have certainly changed over the years! There's an old print in the back bedroom at Glebe Cottage, where I live, of the Durham ox that toured the country in 1809. It was such a famous, prodigious beast that 2000 folk like my great–great–grandfather bought prints of him to stick on their walls. Then, of course, there was the famous Bradwell ox from Essex that weighed two tons. He was six years old, mind, and would have needed to have a longish spell in the stewpot to make him edible by modern standards.

It wouldn't do these days. Jack Spratt's wife liked fat on her beef, but today's housewife wants lean, tender meat, and the rosettes seem to go to animals with some French Charolais in their breeding. To my mind, though, if it's *taste* you're after, you can't beat Aberdeen Angus or Hereford. It's the fat, after all, that gives flavour to the meat.

A mild December, they used to say, was a very unhealthy thing, and folk would shake their heads and talk about a green Christmas and a full churchyard. Mild weather often means damp at this time of year and when I was a lad poorly heated cottages had condensation halfway up their walls and that led to a number of evils from rheumatism to tuberculosis (which was what killed my father in 1924). At Brookfield we stuffed corn husks between the joists of the floorboards to stop the draught whistling through and my mother used to sit me and my brothers in front of the kitchen fire once a week and rub goose grease into our chests. It was horrible, sticky stuff, and we groaned and grumbled like anything, but grumbling didn't do any good. My mum had a will of iron when it came to things she reckoned would keep us healthy.

We didn't suffer, though, as badly as Rosemary Wynyard, an Ambridge lass who lost her chance of a husband because of her mum's faith in animal fats as a cure–all. Rosemary and her twin sister Polly were known everywhere as 'The Beauties' and they were both setting their caps at Tom Whipple, the carter's lad. What he'd done to deserve their attention nobody could make out, because he was an ordinary–looking boy who didn't say or do much beyond scratching the back of his neck with a bit of barley straw. This was in 1919, I should think, the winter after I started walking out with Doris. Once a fortnight, Tom Whipple's boss would let him take a wagonette over to the dance in Penny Hassett hall, and all of us young folk would dress up in our best clothes and pile in for something like twopence each.

Thinking back to the wagonette, it was the autumn I remember best, when Doris and I were just getting to know each other, bumping along the track through the stubble field, with a big hunter's moon shining down, and the girls squealing and clutching the chaps if a barn owl or bat swooped near us. We'd be singing songs from the war – 'Pack up your troubles', 'We're here because we're here', and Joe Grundy's dad, George, would sing 'Mademoiselle from Armentières', waving his stone cider jug about, and me and Walter used to have to stop him when he got to the vulgar bits. We used to sing Doris's favourite song as well:

> Just down the lane
> Over the style
> Under the old oak tree;
> When the clock's striking nine
> And the stars brightly shine,
> There's somebody waiting for me.

She was so fond of that song that she tried to make me meet her of an evening under the oak tree in the field next to Hollowtree Lane, and proper daft I felt, standing there while anybody who passed gave me a peculiar look. In the end Mr Judge, the tenant at Bull Farm, came up to me in the village and said he had seen me poking round his oak tree with a stick three times and what the devil did I mean by it. After that I insisted on meeting Doris on the village green.

A song George Grundy knew, by the way, was 'Good Old Raspberry', which was supposed to be about the head keeper, Davis, who had a huge red nose through drinking. We all used to join in with great enjoyment except for poor Doris, whose dad was an underkeeper. She used to sit quiet and embarrassed, not that the song was terrible!

> Good Old Raspberry
> He's got a boko for three.
> Oh my! What a disgrace!
> Blinking great lump
> Sticking out on his face.
> What would it cost to paint it?
> Oh, doesn't it shine?
> It would make a very good light
> On the Hollerton railway line!

Anyway, it was in December that poor Rosemary Wynyard had her tragedy. She and her sister Polly were quite demented over Tom Whipple by this time. When he turned round on the wagonette and gave them a sort of slow, lazy smile they used to moan out loud, till Doris and some of the older girls told them to behave themselves. At the dancing they wouldn't let him out of their sight, each 'beauty' determined to stop the other one from getting him on his own for even ten minutes.

Just before the Christmas Dance, though, Rosemary got a very bad sore throat, and her mum said she'd got to wear a stocking stuffed full of bacon fat round her neck and no argument. It was quite a popular remedy in Ambridge at that time. Well, Rosemary agreed, and off

47

she and Polly went down to the wagonette, which was waiting outside The Bull, where Rosemary quickly took the stocking off and stuffed it into her bag. Just then, though, her mum jumped out from somewhere screaming, 'You sly devil, you get that stocking back on,' and Rosemary screamed, 'I can't go to a dance with a stocking full of bacon round me neck,' and her mum screamed, 'Well you can come home then,' and dragged her off.

By the New Year, Tom Whipple and Polly were engaged. They were married at Easter 1920 and Rosemary was the sorriest–looking bridesmaid you have ever seen.

Embrocation was another thing folk used to swear by in those days. 'Elliman's Embrocation', and they would even buy the horse variety believing it to be so much stronger and therefore better value for money. The curious thing is, though, that a horse's skin is thinner than human skin, and horse embrocation is generally milder than the human sort!

The strongest belief was in badger fat. The finest badger I ever saw was killed by Pat Fields, the keeper who took Davis's job on the estate in the early thirties. I came across him one December day near Cuckoo Covert, and he had this dead badger lying next to him on top of the ditch. Near it was the vicious wire snare he had used to catch it, the broken strands showing how hard the badger had fought to escape. I told him what a fine animal I thought it was, and he said, 'Fine? Oh it's fine but I wish I'd caught this 'un in October when the blackberries were on the bushes. That's when badgers are at their fattest.'

I have always been fond of badgers myself, and as a farmer I have never found that they do any harm. But Pat Fields wouldn't have it. 'Worse than foxes for chicken and they'll burrow anywhere. There's no good in badgers.' He was going to skin the animal – 'Might get a couple of bob' – and take home some badger steaks, which were said to make a tasty meal, though I never tried it. But what he really wanted the badger for was its fat, which he planned to scrape from the glands on either side of the base of its tail. 'Strong?' he told me, 'it's so strong you can put a lump on your chest and watch your hair standing on end, or if you puts a bit on top of your head you can taste it. Strong? It's no use keeping it in tins, it eats through tins. You have to keep it in a bottle and then be careful it doesn't climb the sides.'

We got our first machine at Brookfield in 1947, and I don't know who was more upset by it, the cows or Simon Cooper. *They* objected to the noise of the Lister petrol engine, the look of the rubber tubes, the steady purr of the vacuum pump and the hiss of air through the teat cups which we fitted awkwardly to their udders. In response they rolled their eyes, kicked over buckets, lifted their tails, and shot dung everywhere. Simon's response was to stand aghast in the corner of the cow parlour. 'They'll all slip their calves,' he said. 'They'll get bad quarters. It'll make their milk as poor as water and they'll all dry off.'

In the end the cows were reconciled to the machine a lot easier than Simon was. I thought of him, the other day, when I looked into the parlour to see the new computerized feeding and automatic cluster removal equipment in operation.

David was milking, and I sidled into the parlour as quietly and unobtrusively as I possible could. The cattle are easily unsettled by a stranger and it's not difficult to upset the cowman, even if he is your own grandson.

To anyone who has not seen a modern herringbone parlour it is not the easiest of contraptions to describe. Basically, it is two platforms with a pit running between them. The cowman works from the pit, and the cows stand on platforms at an angle to the walls on either side. From above, to a short–sighted bird at any rate, it looks a bit like the backbone of a herring!

Parlours can be of varying size to suit the number of cows. Brookfield has room for sixteen, eight on each side, and as I slipped in out of the dark another batch was moving in ready to be milked. David stood at the far end of the parlour, and as each cow went past he read off the number branded on its backside and tapped it out on a little keyboard. This is his latest 'toy', and he gave me a challenging smile as he caught sight of me, as if to say, 'It really does work, Grandad! And it *is* worth all the money.'

What the gadget does is to store in its memory each cow's number and the amount of concentrates she is to be fed, and as she reaches her stall the nuts come rattling down a pipe into the trough in front of her. She gets exactly the right number of pounds (or rather kilograms these days) to match her yield of milk. I stood and watched for a bit and it really did seem to be working! Not that it can do the thinking for itself, David or Graham or Phil has to put the information in once a month (or more frequently at this time of year when they're busy calving) after each cow's milk has been recorded, bearing in mind the cow's potential.

They may know that Mabel (or number thirty–three as she is conveniently known) is capable of giving a bit more if she's fed a little bit extra, whereas Daffodil will do just as well with slightly less.

Having proved the effectiveness of his electronic gadgetry, with all the cows tucking into their nuts, David started to wash each cow's udder with water from one of a number of sprinklers installed in the pit, massaging each udder to encourage the cow to let down her milk. Then he dried them with paper drawn from a huge roll, using a separate piece for each udder to avoid any possibility of spreading disease, and then he drew a little foremilk from each teat to make sure there was no sign of the dreaded mastitis.

While all this was going on, the eight cows on the other side of the pit were being milked and, as each one's udder emptied, a spring–loaded arm removed the teat cups, and left them suspended in the air. This is David's other new device, and he spared a moment to shoot me a quick grin as the cluster on the cow immediately in front of him was whisked off. A moment later, he was dipping the teat cups in sterilizing solution and putting them on the cow opposite, and a couple of seconds later he was back with the cow that had finished milking, dipping its teats in disinfectant to ward off mastitis.

When all eight cows on one side were finished he pressed a button to open the gate and off they went for a supper of silage pulled from the clamp (the so–called self–feed system) before spending the night in individual cubicles. In the meantime, David had pressed a button to let in the next eight cows, and was starting to tap out numbers again on his little machine. . . .

During all this my mind had drifted back sixty years and more, to the tranquillity of the old cowshed at Brookfield when I was young. Milking machines were unheard of (though not unthought of – an early machine was given a silver medal by the Royal Agricultural Society several years before I was born) and I must have been eight or nine when I made my first attempt to milk a cow by hand. I was pestering old Josh, who did the milking when my dad wasn't there, to let me have a go, and in the end he set me to milk Dolly, a cow with teats small enough for my childish hands to cope with. There I sat, proud as Punch, on my three-legged stool, and stuck my head into the cow's flank as I had seen the others do. I got on fine for some time, but then my hands started to ache, so I got up to give them a rest, leaving the bucket with six inches of milk in it under the cow. Dolly, as I dare say you've guessed, promptly kicked the bucket over. I got a clip round the ear from an enraged Josh and left the cowhouse in tears, but I was too proud to complain to my mother, so I took my catapult into the orchard for the rest of the morning to take it out on the starlings.

My father kept about fourteen cows in those Edwardian days, and the number didn't vary much until after the Second World War, when we got the milking machine installed. It doesn't seem many these days, when herds of 200 are not all that uncommon, but believe me, if you had to milk them by hand, on your own, it was more than enough! It took about an hour and a half – ten cows an hour was considered a reasonable rate. That's about the same time it takes David and Graham to get through the 110 cows we have at Brookfield now. The milking machine doesn't milk them any quicker, it just milks eight at a time!

I always enjoyed milking by hand, especially on a cold winter's morning, nuzzling up against the cow and hearing the harsh metallic twang as the first jets of milk hit the bottom of the bucket and then the soft hiss as the froth built up on the milk. Then there was the satisfaction of carrying a nearly full bucket down to the dairy, lifting it above your head and pouring it slowly into the tank. I enjoyed watching it, as it ran over the cooler's corrugations and trickled into the seventeen-gallon churn beneath.

Of course, we had our difficult cows and our ways of dealing with them. The kickers which had to be hobbled, the slow milkers, and the ones with warty teats. There was old Bluebell, who would only let her milk down for Josh – she was all right when he was there, but the very devil to deal with when he was laid up or had a day off. But we put up with all their quirks and peccadilloes if they milked well. Nowadays any cow that will not conform is replaced pretty quickly – you can't keep fifteen milkers hanging round outside the parlour just because one cow is playing up.

In my day, once the cows came in for the winter they were chained by the neck in the same stall until they went out again the following April, and we acted as waiters, nursemaids and lavatory attendants to them, making sure that their hay racks and troughs were

52

replenished, shovelling away the muck, and tucking them up on a good bed of straw at night.

It is easy, of course, now that my working days are over, to look back fondly to those 'good old times'. I know that I shan't be called upon again to put in the back-breaking effort it sometimes involved! But I also wonder if David, as he lets out his last batch of cows, sets the cleansing solution circulating through the pipes and starts hosing down the parlour, gets as much fulfilment from it all as I used to, when I strawed down my little herd and wished them good night.

JANUARY

I EARNED my first money when I was seven years old, killing rats with Walter Gabriel and selling them to the Parish Council for a penny each. He was a funny, sentimental little chap was Walter and he desperately wanted a shilling to buy a present for his sister Alice. Some awful accident, it seemed, had befallen the china doll she'd been given for Christmas.

'I so want her to be happy,' said Walter, 'and there's rats bigger'n cats at Burminton Hovel.'

'Do they pay more for fat 'uns?' I asked, ready to believe anything of the marvellous, munificent 'Rook and Rat' club that had just been started in the village.

'Not that I've heard of,' said Walter, puffing away, as always, on a empty clay pipe his uncle had given him, 'but fat 'uns can't run so fast, can they?'

Anyway, he borrowed his dad's terrier and stick (without asking I'm sure) and off we went to Burminton Hovel, which was a barn on Home Farm land standing next to a rick of corn waiting to be threshed. It was biting cold, with lots of slushy ice about and the soil was like glue as we crept over a ploughed field. I was wearing my corduroy knickerbockers, but Walter was wearing short trousers and he had tied string round each leg, just above his knees, to stop the rats jumping up and gnawing at his private parts!

In the event we managed to stir up a couple of dozen rats, or the terrier did, and we chased round after them. I think we had killed one each and the terrier had accounted for four when Walter accidentally thwacked his stick down on the dog, who tried to bite him, and an estate worker came in swearing and threatening to tell our dads about us.

I am afraid I seemed to spend most of my boyhood being led astray by Walter. He was four months older than I was, you see, and that gave him a permanent advantage when it came to wordly experience. I was quite a backward lad in some ways, I don't suppose I puffed a clay pipe till I was ten!

That night we took our dead rats down to the Ambridge Reading Room, where the parish clerk (so a notice outside told us) was authorized to receive vermin between the hours of 5 p.m. and 8 p.m. every Saturday. Although neither Walter nor I realized it, 'Rook and Rat' clubs were springing up in many villages at that time. They were paid money by the new parish councils, that came in around the turn of the century, and Borchester District Council even issued a list of recommended payments. In 1903 they suggested three pence a dozen for house sparrows and finches, four pence a dozen for starlings, and a penny each for rooks and rats. In summer they suggested payment of a penny for rooks' eggs. It was the following year that Silas Winter fell out of one of our elm trees at Brookfield while trying to reach a rook's nest and broke his arm. 'I'll break the other one if you try that again,' my dad told him.

It must be one of my most vivid childhood memories, the sight of the Ambridge Reading Room on that January night. There were about six oil lamps burning for a start, which struck me as wonderful extravagance, and by their light the parish clerk was sitting with a little pile of dead rats next to him and rooks and starlings strung up on poles. Around him, on benches and at a long pine table, were men of the village, playing quoits and bagatelle, or poring over copies of the *Daily Graphic* and the *London Mail*. On either side of the roaring fire, under a portrait of the Squire and his wife and with a huge brass spitoon between them, were old Mumford and young Mumford, the village undertaker and his son.

Old Mumford, with his huge grey beard and rheumy eyes was the oldest man in the village, and was said to be well over seventy. There had been three brothers at one time, but one died of fever and the other went to be a soldier and was killed in the Meerut Massacre. Old Mumford (who wasn't old at all, then, of course) was left to run the undertaking and carpentry business himself, till his son grew up to help him. They were good carpenters, the Mumfords, and there's a Mumford wheelbarrow on display now at the Churcham Farm Museum. But for miles around, in those days, 'a job for Mumford' meant that somebody had died, and either Mumford or his son would soon be measuring the corpse with their length of black rope, knotting it once for the length and again for the width.

Both Mumfords were renowned for the way they selected coffin wood with beautiful grain markings, and for their skill at curving the coffin sides by partially sawing the grain on the inside and softening the outer grain with boiling water. Few village coffin-makers managed anything better than a straight-sided box.

Mumfords were terribly expensive, though, and also terribly mean. The reason old Mumford wouldn't die, they said, was because he couldn't bear the thought of paying his own firm's funeral charges! Anyway, there he was by the fire on that January night, staring vacantly around him. I looked up at him with awe, a little lad couldn't believe that anyone could grow so old.

Walter demanded our money from the parish clerk. There were a few laughs, and a joke or two at our expense, but we got our sixpence and scuttled out into the night; Walter back to the forge where his dad was still working, and me back over the icy fields to Brookfield. As I said, I was only seven, and my mother thought I had gone out to the stables to wait for my father to come home from Borchester.

The Reading Room lasted until the mid–twenties, and was a remarkable institution when you think about it.

Farm labourers and village tradesmen used to pay a shilling a quarter to belong during the winter (it was closed during the summer) and would go along each evening to play games and to read a selection of papers and magazines. There were two reasons, I believe, for its popularity during Edwardian times. The Temperance Movement was very strong in those days, and there were several 'Chapel' families in the village. There was also the great faith, among all sorts of folk, in the virtues of education. Ordinary people were learning to read and write properly for the first time and labourers would take great pride in being able to decipher the columns of the *Birmingham Gazette* or *The London Illustrated News*. The vicar and school teacher even used to set them all a monthly essay competition, on a subject of topical interest, and organize a weekly 'quiz' to test their knowledge of current events.

The idea of working men – labourers, bootmakers, wainwrights and farriers – meeting of an evening to answer an essay competition seems both sad and comical nowadays. It is difficult, even for me, to remember the feeling of *hope*, and belief in a bright future, that existed among all types of folk in the years up till 1914.

On New Year's Day, our Phil retires to the farm office and isn't seen again for the next six weeks. That's a bit of an exaggeration, of course, he has to sit on the bench once a week, see his bank manager once or twice and fit in the odd day's shooting, but January and often the first half of February are spent planning, ordering and discussing all the operations which go into running a modern mixed farm.

The traditional New Year's Day start has become something of a family joke. 'You can't disturb your father, he's thinking,' Elizabeth used to be told. Shula, with her usual frankness, claims that her dad disappears into the office to recover from his hangover from the night before! I suppose the custom *could* have begun in that way!

The office at Brookfield, as on many farms, is attached to the house but is not really a part of it. Ours used to be the dairy in the days when we had the old cowhouse. If you go to the back door of the farmhouse and turn left you find yourself in the kitchen; if you turn right and pick your way over an assortment of gumboots, sticks, halters, buckets and drums of chemicals, you find yourself at the farm office.

Oddly enough, the inside has hardly changed at all since I handed everything over to Phil twenty-odd years ago. The centrepiece is still an old roll-top desk which hasn't been rolled for fifty years. I remember buying it at a sale in the thirties, when farming began to look up a bit, and for a few months I conscientiously rolled down the top every time I had finished using it. It wasn't long, though, before bits began to stick out and make the operation difficult! Nowadays, the pigeonholes are stuffed so full I don't think you could get the top down more than a few inches – if, indeed, it still rolls at all.

The chair is the same swivel-backed one with the horsehair sticking out of the seat. There is a telephone of course, a typewriter, a moisture tester for the grain, and sundry spare parts doing temporary duty as paper weights. There's a wall diary that came from Rodway and Watson, the auctioneers, and last time I looked in there was a rather cheeky calendar on the back of the door that David must have put up; it certainly didn't look the sort a magistrate would put on his wall!

About the only noticeable additions made since my day are a calculator and a filing cabinet; elsewhere it is undisguised chaos, with piles of magazines, cuttings and leaflets; stacked wherever there is room. From this highly unlikely setting, our Phil now runs a successful business with a turnover of getting on for a quarter of a million pounds a year.

One day, I suppose, David will talk his dad into getting a computer. Brian has one up at Home Farm and swears by it but then, if you've been talked into spending several thousand pounds on something, you're not likely to admit you made a mistake. The computer got me into trouble, though, last New Year's Day.

We were all having our tea in the sitting–room, and Jennifer had laid on a marvellous spread, as usual, with baked ham, and a Dundee cake and sausages for the younger children. Jennifer and Brian themselves were particularly enjoying a salad made with smoked salmon, lobster claws and asparagus. That was when Mrs Perkins remembered how her first Arthur had nearly died after swallowing a live oyster at Southend, and started telling Brian all about it. 'Come on, Dan!' he said, after a bit. 'You wanted to know what the computer can do, so I'll show you!'

Jennifer asked him, couldn't it wait, but he was up and off, and I had to follow him to the farm office with a slice of cake in my hand. 'Interested in sheep?' he said, when he had switched it on. 'Well just look at this.' He pressed a button and rows and rows of figures appeared. Then he tapped out something onto his little keyboard and pressed the button again, and a fresh lot of figures ran across the screen. 'That,' he said, 'is what happens if the lamb price is up one penny a kilo in July.'

'Goodness me,' I said, trying to sound impressed, and wondering what would happen to his 'projections' if he got a nasty bout of abortion before then. Could his computer predict that? I was just going to ask him when Jennifer called to say that Sammy Whipple was at the back door and he dashed off. A minute later, just as I was finishing up my cake, the door opened and little Kate came running in shouting, 'Grandpa, I've found you!' and jumped on my knee.

I suppose Peggy was right, I ought to have known better than let a child of six play about with expensive machinery. But small children do seem to move so very *fast* these days, and besides, she seemed to know exactly what she was doing. I'd hardly blinked before she was pressing buttons and making figures flash on and off, and a moment later she put a cassette into a tape recorder and a message came up on the screen: 'I've thought of a number, Kate,' the computer said. 'Now you just guess what it is.'

'You try, Grandpa!' said Kate, still wriggling about on my knee, and when I said 'Ninety-six, because that was the year I was born', she pressed 'ninety-six' and the computer said, 'No, Kate, that's much too high. Try again.'

We were still playing half an hour later when Brian came back. 'Aha, playing that game I see!' he said, cheerfully, and then, more thoughtfully, 'she didn't mess about with anything before she put the cassette on, did she?'

It turned out that Kate had pressed 'Enter' or something like that, and fed lots of bits of gobbledegook into Brian's 'floppy-disc', whatever that is. Bits of nonsense were still flashing up on the screen weeks later, and I was still getting reproachful looks from him as late as April.

I suppose Brian's computer is progress, though, just as it was progress for me to buy that roll-top desk in the early thirties. My dad's system had been 'the clock'. When he received cheques he paid them straight into the bank (Phil and his friends might think they've invented 'cash flow problems' – they haven't), but everything else that came through the post or by hand went behind the clock on the kitchen mantelpiece. It was only when the clock was threatening to fall over, or somebody came knocking on the door for his money, that Dad sorted through the rest.

Anyway, in January, our Phil sits quietly in his lair, catching up on back numbers of magazines he is sent whether he asks for them or not, thinking of the mistakes he made last year and what he can do to avoid them this season, and ringing up the grain merchant and the machinery dealer. Now and again he bursts into the kitchen shouting, 'Guess what they're asking for nitrogen?' He doesn't really expect Jill to guess. He just wants a cup of coffee. Occasionally, he and David go into a huddle with a calculator. Should they consider introducing some Holstein blood into the herd, which will mean more milk but less beef? Will the increase in the milk cheque make up for the drop in the calf price? They might wonder about getting a better bulk tank; the leaflet will come out and the small ads will be gone though in case there's a second-hand one around; a telephone call or two will be made.

I like to see the two of them working together on these occasions, with David nudging for things to be done, and Phil having to restrain his enthusiasm without discouraging him too much. It reminds me of conversations that took place in that selfsame office thirty years ago!

They used to call him the 'bull in a bowler hat' when artificial insemination came in forty years ago, and the AI man started visiting farms in his little van. I don't know where the bowler hat came from, unless it referred to the Ministry of Agriculture's close involvement with the scheme.

What an awful fuss it all caused! Simon Cooper was convinced that cows inseminated artificially instead of being served by a bull (the way Nature intended!) would give birth to calves with two heads or else fail to breed altogether. When the Andersons started using AI in their herd at Penny Hassett, just after the Second World War, their land girl left. Her father, it turned out, was a vicar and absolutely refused to allow her to become involved in unnatural practices such as these.

Well, I've lived to see them all confounded. There's no doubt that we now have our best herd of cows ever at Brookfield, and the country is just about drowning in milk.

We use the AI service a lot at this time of year – and a marvellous service it is, too. By simply telephoning the local AI centre Phil can order semen from the best Friesian bulls in the country, or any other breed for that matter. He can ring at two o'clock in the morning if he likes and simply leave his name and address and the name of the bull he wants on the answering machine. Sure enough the AI man will drive into the yard the next morning and inseminate the cow. It costs only a few pounds, and it's available every day of the year except Christmas Day. They do their best to reach you through snow, floods or ice. One year, 1963 I think it was, we towed the chap and his van down from Wharton's Garage, across the frozen fields, and then towed him back afterwards.

Mind you, it's in our interest to get the AI man there if there's a cow ready for him. David was telling me the other day that we lose about £30 every time a cow is 'missed'. Every dairy farmer, you see, aims to get each of his cows to calve once a year. That gives him nine or ten months' milking and a couple of months' rest before they calve again. About six weeks after the cow has calved the farmer looks to see if she's ready for the bull again. The trouble is that if he misses her coming into season he has to wait three weeks before she comes on heat again. That means her next calf will come three weeks later and the long-term cost, according to David, is £30.

One way you know a cow's coming on heat is when you see other cows trying to mount her. Everyone on the farm is encouraged to keep an eye open. 'I think seventy-one's coming on!' you'll hear Neil or Jethro shouting to Graham, and he will hurry off to check for himself. These days most dairy farms rely on AI, although most of them do keep a beef bull to use on cows they don't want to breed from. Phil uses a Hereford because it always leaves the offspring with a white face, and that makes them easy to sell, because everyone knows what breed the father was.

It's a long-term business, dairy farming. After the AI

man has done his job it's nine months before the calf arrives, and if it's a heifer there's a further two and half years before it, in turn, has a calf and starts milking. This was one of the facts that surprised a party of schoolchildren we had round Brookfield last summer. Jill and David had cobbled up a simple information sheet telling them that we had 110 cows and that they each gave an average yield of just over 1,100 gallons in a lactation, which was nearly 10,000 pintas! She also told them that a cow drinks up to fifteen gallons of water a day (but avoided mentioning that milk itself contains nearly eighty-eight per cent water).

I am ofter paraded on these occasions as an example of a 'real old farmer' and I keep threatening to wear a smock and a big spotted-red handkerchief round my neck, but I enjoy myself, I suppose, and last summer I told the youngsters that the most milk a cow had ever produced in a lifetime was 36,211 gallons, a fact I had gleaned from looking through a farming almanac. I was totally stumped, though, when one lad shouted from the back, 'What's that in litres, mister?'

There's only been one winter, that I remember, when barn owls hunted by day in their desperation for food and thrushes could be found huddled in groups, frozen dead on the branches of the thorn trees. That was 1947. My old farm-record book tells me that a hard frost set in on 27 January and remained, unbroken, until 14 March.

It was the sheep, of course, that gave us our biggest headache. The cows were under cover and snug enough, but the ewes were out in the yard, protected only by a few hurdles in the shelter of straw bales that were themselves frozen solid. We lost fewer lambs than might be expected, mind you. A few, born at night and separated from their mothers, were killed swiftly by the cold. One had its eyes ripped out by a carrion crow that swooped down in broad daylight (Phil blasted at it with a shotgun from his bedroom window, but it was too late).

In the kitchen, though, Doris kept the orphan lambs and the sickly ones in cardboard boxes in front of the stove and most of them pulled through.

The problem as the cold kept its grip, was how to give the sheep some exercise. 'They'll have snow-sickness afore long,' Simon kept saying, looking at the miserable ewes all jammed up together on one side of the yard. Snow-sickness – or twin-lambs disease as it's often known – is usually caused by sheep not being able to get proper food, and their unborn lambs draining away vital nutrients, but lack of exercise might have something to do with it.

In the end we ran the ewes out of the yard and down the track, laboriously cleared by Blossom and Boxer pulling a makeshift snowplough, and then back up the track again to the yard. I don't know what the ewes thought we were up to. They're not the most intelligent of animals, but they must have thought it very funny behaviour.

One day, in late February I think it was, we had a few days of clear blue sky and sunshine. I took a risk and moved about two dozen sheep over to Pikey Piece, where they could scrabble around some exposed grass, poor as it was, and where they were protected by a small covert. That night it snowed, harder and thicker than ever. In the morning there were drifts up to the bedroom window on the end gable of the house. I called Phil out of bed. He was a lazy blighter at eighteen and stayed under the blankets till eight o'clock if his mum let him. We pulled on our knee-length socks, gumboots and greatcoats and set off for Pikey Piece. Nothing! Not a sheep or a hurdle in sight. Just a great drift of snow against the blackthorn hedge that ran down from the covert.

It was Phil who found them. He waded through the snow on the top of the drift until he spotted three of four small holes in the snow beneath. That was where the sheep were breathing, and a few moments later we had dug the first one out. It was a bigger job than it seemed, though. Phil ran back to the house for shovels and came back with his mum and Christine, and we all set to work. The sheep were buried in a line along the hedge. They were pretty hungry when we got them out, but otherwise seemed to regard being buried alive as all part of a day's work.

By early March, birds and wild animals were suffering very badly indeed. Christine, who was fifteen, came into the house in tears one morning. She had pulled back the canvas from the hay bales and found a small flock of blue-tits frozen dead beneath it. Another day, walking by the Am, I came across a grey heron, his legs broken and embedded in the ice. In the kale field you could see where rabbits were tunnelling under the snow and feeding on the crop. You could see the vicious little trails where the stoats and weasels were following and killing them.

It was a terrible winter, but also a very beautiful one. Huge icicles hung down from the trees, and in one place where the Am tumbled over a fallen tree the spray was frozen into an amazing shape and shone green and gold in the sunshine. One morning, Tom took me along the riverbank by the deerpark to a patch of open water which he and the other two keepers kept clear of ice. All animals and birds have to drink and there were footprints of foxes, badgers, hares, rabbits, common rats, weasels. . . just about every animal of the fields and woods, together with the prints of moorhens, herons, wild duck, partridge and pheasant. At night it must have been like an African watering-hole. We wondered if the thirsty animals forgot their enmity for a moment as they crowded to the river-bank. It was a fanciful thought, but Tom said no, the different animals must have come to drink at different times, the poor and the weak having to wait until all was clear.

We only keep a few hens at Brookfield nowadays. A lot of farmers have given them up altogether and buy their eggs from a neighbour or even from the supermarket. I suppose it's a sign of the times – most farmers buy their milk in bottles, after all – but to my mind, a farm's not a proper place without a few hens pecking about the yard. I know they can be a wretched nuisance, and there isn't much, if anything, in the way of profit, but they do bring the place to life and make a farm look like a farm and not some sort of rural factory site.

Back in the thirties, it's worth remembering, it was the humble hen that helped see many a small farmer through the depression. When Doris and I were struggling through our worst years at Brookfield, the income from the hens was a very important matter. We debated over the different types, the way we debate over breeds of cattle or sheep these days. Light Sussex were my favourites, but Doris always swore by White Leghorns. She said they gave more eggs and ate less, and she was right, but they didn't give you much in the way of a tasty dinner when they'd finished their 'working lives' as egg layers. The Leghorn had a thin, scrappy carcase, but the Light Sussex was a big, meaty bird, lovely to look at when it was alive and providing a beautiful delicious 'cut-and-come-again' fowl when it reached the table.

Between the wars we kept our hens on free range in the Little Field by the house, but we lost a terrible lot to foxes and in the end we went in for the arks which were becoming all the rage. These were triangled-shaped huts with a little run attached. They gave the benefit of free range and also security from Charlie. You still see these arks from time to time and it wouldn't surprise me to see them come back into fashion, what with all this interest in 'self-sufficiency'. You had to move them every day, which was a time-consuming nuisance, but the hens always had fresh ground to peck and scratch over, and didn't those eggs taste good!

When people started keeping hens in batteries, the profit went for folk like us. We gradually gave them up until, by the time we left Brookfield, we only had twenty or thirty left. We took those with us to Glebe Cottage and I think our Phil was glad to see the back of them. We had kept them loose round the yard, you see, telling ourselves that they picked up a living for next to nothing, just a handful of corn a day. But Phil grumbled about the damage they did and the corn they pinched, and he used to reckon it was a day's work cleaning three inches of poultry droppings off the binder when he got it out every year to cut the corn. He and Jill did without hens for a few years, but they must have missed them, because there's a couple of dozen back there now. Not Light Sussex, mind you, but one of these new fangled hybrids. They lay eggs like mad, Jill says, but they can't compare to the old breed in appearance.

Poultry scratting round the yard always used to provide 'pin money' for the farmer's wife and, at Brookfield, Doris was jealous of any interference from me. I only tried it once and that was a terrible mistake.

It happened one winter not long after we'd given up keeping hens 'seriously'. The previous summer Doris had set a clutch of eggs to provide replacement pullets, and another hen had managed to bring off a sitting in a clump of nettles. The result was that, by January, we had thirty hens spreading straw round the yard and wreaking havoc in the kitchen garden, instead of the usual fifteen.

'Something'll have to be done,' I told Doris firmly, but she told me to bother my head about cows and sheep and 'never mind my hens, thank you, Dan Archer.' By the end of the month, the hens were still the same in number. Fred Barratt and I decided on direct action. We'd been sitting chewing the fat round the fire at Brookfield all evening, making a mess of a half-bottle of whisky in the process, and Fred claimed to be an expert at the 'finger test' – an infallible method, said Fred, of telling whether a bird was laying or not. All you had to do was to see if you could get two fingers between the pelvic bones of the bird. If you could, she was laying. If you couldn't, she wasn't, and in that case she ought to be packed off to Borchester Market.

Fortified by the whisky Fred and I sallied out into the cold winter air. We found an old crate and went to the machinery shed, where I knew the birds were roosting. After that there was half an hour of chaos, with Fred flashing a torch briefly to show where hens were perched on beams, then me clambering over the baler in pitch dark to grab them. 'Well she's not laying for certain,' Fred would say, applying his famous finger test to each hysterical hen I caught, and into the crate it would go. In the end we had ten hens in the crate and the place in pandemonium with birds clucking indignantly and the cock crowing his head off in the dark. Bruised but triumphant, Fred and I went back to the house for a well-earned night cap.

Doris was a bit tight-lipped about it, but she couldn't really complain. Old birds that are past laying have to be got rid of, she knew that well enough. Next morning after milking, I set off to Borchester Market with the crate of hens and even before I'd unloaded them a chap offered me five bob apiece. I took the money, feeling more than a little pleased with myself, did my other business and off home I went with half a pound of chocolate caramels as a present for Doris.

That was when I got a nasty shock. 'Caramels?' shouted Doris, standing at the back door all pink in the face. 'Don't talk to me about caramels, where are my pullets?'

It turned out that the birds I had taken to market were not old hens gone off, but two old hens and eight pullets which weren't due to start laying for another month. That was why they had failed Fred's famous finger test!

I had to go straight back to the market and buy six point-of-lay pullets at eighteen shillings apiece. Fred laughed himself silly in The Bull that night. 'You didn't tell me there were any *pullets*,' he kept saying, but I couldn't raise much of a smile. The episode had cost me a small fortune, particularly considering the price of best-quality chocolate caramels.

FEBRUARY

SOMETIME in February Nature starts up business again. It may be earlier on, it may be later, but I can't recall a year yet when there wasn't a hint of spring somewhere in the month. It might be the rhubarb sprouting in the garden, or the elder buds bursting in the hedge or it might be the daffodils pushing up an inch and more in a week and the nettles starting to grow in the orchard. One Sunday I'll go to Evensong and the grass by the churchyard path will be green and empty, the next Sunday it will be covered in thousands of snowdrops, not bending their heads yet, of course, but pointing them up to the sky like tiny spears.

In the old days folk used to get very worked up about the weather we got in February. Fine weather, they said, was a terrible thing, and there must be more rhymes about Candlemas Day than there are about St Swithin's. The best known in our part of the world is:

> If Candlemas be fair and bright
> Winter will have another flight.
> But if Candlemas Day be wild and rain
> Winter be gone and won't come again.

Another rhyme Tom Forrest told me once was,

> 'Warm and sunny on Candlemas Day
> Saddle your horse and go buy hay.'

It's all a lot of nonsense, though, as far as I can make out. I've known a sunny Candlemas followed by an early

69

spring and a wet, cold Candlemas that carried on being wet and cold for months.

To me a fine, springlike day in February is just a welcome promise of things to come. Not that farmers can afford to relax, mind you. At the beginning of the month the dairy farmer still has more than a third of winter ahead of him. His cows came in halfway through October and they probably won't go out again until the second week of April, no matter how springlike the weather is. There's often an anxious look in the silage clamp to see how far the cows have eaten, reflecting, if you like, a more sensible country rhyme:

> The Farmer should have by Candlemas Day
> Half his straw and half his hay.

The days are getting longer, which is cheering in itself. At some point in the month the land may be fit to work and there'll be a day or two when the midges come out. Meanwhile the keen chaps are out putting nitrogen on their crops to pep things up after the hard weather. It works wonders on winter wheat that's turned a bit yellow, and as a tonic for oilseed rape. Later in the month, the fertilizer spinner will be at work on the grass to encourage an early bite. The dairy farmer is an optimist, you see, and can always remember that year when he was able to turn his cows out in the last week of March. Most seasons the February nitrogen is washed down the nearest ditch or the east winds keep the grass in check anyway, but there's always the chance of something better *this* year.

I was standing in the yard at Brookfield the other day, warm and snug outside in my new overcoat, watching a twenty-ton grain lorry being filled with a load of wheat and thinking about the way we used to do things and what back-breaking work it always was hauling sacks of corn up into the granary. I hadn't noticed our Phil in the

70

farm office until he opened the window and called out, 'What the devil are you standing out *there* for, dad?' and I called back, 'I'm waiting for the threshing machine, Phil!' – making a joke, you see, because it was always in the second week of February that the thresher used to come to us. Phil looked a bit startled and said, 'Oh, I see,' and shut the window. Then he sat there watching me with a worried look on his face. Wondering if my woolly scarf was properly wrapped round my neck, I suppose.

It must be more than thirty years since a threshing machine came to Brookfield. At the end it was hauled to the farm by a huge Field Marshall tractor, but before that, between the wars, it would come lumbering into the yard behind a steam traction engine, a living monster of a thing (so Jack and Phil reckoned when they were little) that hooted and hissed and blew out clouds of steam. Before the traction engine, when I was a lad, the threshing was done by a 'portable' engine, that was pulled from farm to farm by horses, with its tumbril of coal, the elevator and the threshing drum.

Word would come that the thresher was ready and my father and Josh would go to fetch it over. I can picture them now, on a bright bitter February day in 1910 or 1911, hauling the old iron-wheeled 'portable' into the yard, my brother Frank holding the gate open and my other brother, Ben, astride one of the Shire horses, waving his cap in the air and shouting with excitement. I remember it so vividly, perhaps, because I had a terrible fight with Ben on that day.

They always said of the Archer brothers that Frank was the cleverest and I was the quietest. Ben, well, Ben was the wild one. If anything was happening he had to have a part in it and if he played a game he had to win. I was about fifteen at the time, and he was thirteen. We ended up in a scrap because he wanted *my* place in the threshing team.

There were several jobs involved with threshing. In

71

the first place we had to haul the threshing drum and 'portable' into the rickyard and square them up against one of the ricks. Then, while the engine was being fired, Frank and Ben would go round the rick fixing small-mesh nets to the sides to catch the rats that were gorging themselves on grain inside it. (One winter, though, in the early fifties, just before we bought the combine, it wasn't rats that streamed out of the corn rick but about fifty grey squirrels!) Then, when all was prepared, Josh would stand on the rick with two men behind him. Josh was the key figure, the 'feeder'. When he gave a signal the lever was thrown and the threshing drum began to turn. The thing after that was to keep it fed. What a hungry beast it was! At sixteen I was old enough to take my turn on the rick. The other bloke and I would pass the sheaves to Josh. With a flick of his knife he would cut the twine and send the corn down into the drum.

If you were watching from below, you could admire the rhythm, almost what you might call the *elegance* of blokes working together on a corn rick to feed a threshing machine, but it didn't feel very elegant when you were up there. I can remember praying for the belt to come off, or for a bit of metal to fall into the drum along with a sheaf – anything, in fact, that would bring the whirring monster to a halt for just a moment and give us a breather. Later, of course, when I was 'in charge', I would do anything to avoid a hold-up!

The worst job, though, was clearing away the chaff and that was always reserved for the newest and least experienced member of the team. In other words, Ben. 'T'is the chaff for you,' my dad would say, and poor Ben had to do it whether he liked it or not.

In time Frank was able to take over on the chaff and Ben did get to work on the rick, but he had no patience, hadn't Ben. In the year I'm talking about, he was so enraged with jealousy that he went to the stable loft and when I went in he threw a saddle down on top of me.

Well, I swung up a ladder to get at him and he threw another bit of tack at me. We rolled about that loft punching each other till I walloped him so hard he slid back down the ladder taking the skin off his arm and shoulder and bruising his back something dreadful.

He suffered worse later on though. Corn chaff is horrible stuff. Somebody once said that trying to scoop it up is like trying to pick vinegar up with a fork. Ben's job was to collect it from under the threshing drum in a big sheet, and carry it away to be burned. Chaff, especially when we were doing barley, used to get under the clothes and irritate the skin like nothing else on earth. With his grazed, battered skin, Ben must have suffered agonies that day, but being Ben, he suffered without complaint!

After being threshed, the corn poured down a chute into sacks – and heavy sacks they were too. One man would knee them out onto the scales, where he would add or take away a bit of corn until the weight was correct. Two-and-a-quarter hundredweight for wheat it always was, and two hundredweight for barley.

That compares to the *half*-hundredweight bags that Neil's weaner pellets come in nowadays! No wonder there were so many bad backs among farm workers, because the sacks of corn had to be carried up into the granary, and then heaved down again when the corn was sold.

Whenever I look at those worn, stone granary steps I think of a tale Ned Larkin told me about the first farmer he ever worked for – old Smart from Paunton Farm, who's dead now. After Ned had been there for a couple of years earning thirty bob a week he asked for a rise. 'So you want a rise, do you?' said his boss. 'Well, you come with me, then.' And he took Ned up to the top of the granary steps. 'There,' he said, 'is that high enough for you?'

There aren't too many farmers left like old Smart and the sweat and the labour have gone, thank goodness.

The twenty-ton grain lorry in the yard the other day was being filled by an auger at the rate of half a ton a minute. All our Phil had to do was to keep an eye on things from the farm office, and work out whether or not to sell another load or wait for the price to creep up a bit. I daresay he also wondered what his old dad was doing, standing out there in the cold wind with a daft look on his face!

I can't help having a quiet chuckle when I hear folk talk about 'self-sufficiency'. They write books about it these days, and bring out magazines. There was even a conference about it in Borchester not long ago. Mr Fletcher went, and came back full of ideas for having his own goat for milk and cheese, a couple of lambs, and a garden that would keep him in vegetables all the year round.

'How I envy the man,' he said to Joe Grundy, 'who has the satifaction of living his life from the land. He is a man beholden to nobody.'

'That's true,' said Joe, a bit surprised, 'and thirsty work it all is.'

Mr Fletcher bought him another pint and Joe offered to send Eddie down to Glebelands with a digger and turn the Fletchers' patio into a vegetable plot. 'He doesn't cost much doesn't Eddie,' Joe said, 'and think of all that satisfaction and joy and contentment you'll get from it.'

'What do you think, Mr Archer?' asked Mr Fletcher, turning to me, and I had to tell him, even at the risk of losing Eddie a morning's work, that I had practised 'self-sufficiency' for nearly forty years, and it was darned hard going!

I was exaggerating a bit, perhaps, but you're allowed a little licence at my age. We didn't actually make our own soap or even grind our own flour at Brookfield, but the sort of farming I was born into was a kind of 'self-sufficiency' with a bit of surplus produce to sell. In return for our milk, and our spare calves, lambs and chickens, we usually earned enough to buy in tea, sugar, oil, clothing. . .

It was a real *family* farm in those days. Everybody belonged, everybody had a place and a job to do. We boys were drawn into the labour force as soon as we could walk, almost, helping Mum to pick gooseberries or Dad to scare the rooks off the corn. I was five years old when I had my first morning job of collecting the eggs (and in those days they were laid all over the buildings and round the yard, and had to be sought and discovered with great cunning). From then on there were jobs to do before school, and jobs waiting for me when I got home.

It was a tough life, I suppose, and I might have been unhappy had I been a great scholar and wanted to sit in the corner reading poems. But I don't remember ever feeling hard done by. The children of other tenant farmers were doing the same sort of thing, and we were a sight better off than the labourers' kids. There was no television or records or much in the way of books or magazines, but our time was already occupied. For recreation we learned to ride and to shoot at a very early age.

One thing we were never short of was food. We were literally surrounded by it. There were always raspberries, gooseberries and redcurrants galore in the garden (I often wonder why the birds never pinched them, the way they do at Glebe Cottage nowadays); apples, pears and cherries in the orchard. There were eggs and the occasional chicken, there was the annual pig and all that provided. My father grew a row of potatoes along the headland of one of the fields and the rest of the vegetables came from the kitchen garden. There were hundreds of rabbits waiting to be shot or trapped, and from the dairy there was an abundance of milk, butter, cheese, cream and junket. There was cider to drink, and my mother's home-made wine for special occasions. All in all, I reckon we ate as they do at Home Farm today – even if we didn't have video games!

It was a simple, straightforward way of life and, from the time I was born, it didn't change in forty years. We were a bit better off in the First War, I suppose, when we grew a few more acres of corn, but the size of the dairy herd hardly varied from the turn of the century to the forties. And the dairy herd was the very heart of Brookfield. Our fourteen or fifteen cows earned most of our money, and consumed nearly all of our oats, barley and hay.

There were other things of course. We grew a small field of wheat (although that was mainly so we could have some straw for thatching the hay and corn ricks) and we had a few acres of mangolds and turnips. We had two horses and the mare would give us a foal each year that we would sell once it was broken in. There were generally a couple of sows snuffling round the yard with their litters and there were my mother's hens. There was a cob who pulled the cart to market, raked and turned the hay and (very importantly!) provided my father with an occasional day's hunting.

Our main income came from milk, and when the cows were doing well we were able to send off three or even four churns a day. My father had a contract with a dairy in Birmingham and twice a day the milk would be taken off to the station.

I must have been eleven or twelve, I suppose, when I was first sent off to the station with those two precious churns. I was as proud as Punch, I remember that, and I even managed to get the horse into a trot just as we turned into the yard at Hollerton Junction. 'Mr Daniel Archer's milk for the Birmingham train!' I called to two porters, as I jumped down, importantly, from the cart. They reduced me to instant misery.

'How are you going to get them down off there then?' said one porter, in an interested sort of way, and the other said, 'You saying a lad like you can get them churns down, are you?'

'T'aint our job getting churns down from carts,' said

the first as I stared at them, open-mouthed. 'Dear me, no,' said the second. 'Us ain't allowed to get churns down from carts.'

I climbed into the back of the cart and tried, with every ounce of my strength, to lift one of the churns, but it had seventeen gallons of milk inside it and must have weighed the best part of two-hundredweight. I could hardly move it, let alone lift it! Disaster was overwhelming me as I tugged, red-faced, at the handle, and I think I might very well have burst into tears, twelve years old or not, if those two persons hadn't come forward with grins all over their faces, and swung the churns down for me.

'I don't reckon this lad be ready to take on the farm just yet,' said one. 'No, not *just* yet,' said the other, and they laughed and bowled the churns along the platform as easily as if they'd been two hoops.

Apart from the milk, the only other regular income came from my mother's sale of butter, cream, fruit, poultry, and even flowers. Once a week on market day she would load the trap or the cart if my father had pigs or a calf to sell, and off they would go. While my father was doing his business, and even enjoying a drink with his acquaintances, my mother would sit in the market nattering to the farmers' wives and selling her wares.

It doesn't seem much to get off a hundred-acre farm, when you think about it. Three or four churns of milk a day, the odd chicken, a few pounds of butter and a few eggs. But this was before the days of chemical aids. Yields were low, half a ton of barley to an acre, perhaps, compared to five times that amount now. There were many crop failures to survive, with no weedkillers to stop the charlock from smothering the corn. We couldn't tickle up the odd field with nitrogen to get an early bite of grass, so the cows had to be kept indoors for longer in the spring.

There were seven of us living off the place, including Josh and our other labourer, and if not much went off the farm, very little came in. What we couldn't grow, we did without – and I don't suppose that's the sort of 'self-sufficiency' Mr Fletcher would enjoy!

There's an old calendar on the kitchen wall at Glebe Cottage given to me by Pru Forrest about four years ago, showing a weatherbeaten shepherd leaning on his crook with a bonny lamb under one arm and the ewe standing quietly at his feet looking up lovingly.

Every time our Phil notices it, at this time of year at least, he bursts out laughing. We're coming up to lambing time, you see, and it isn't a bit like it is in my picture!

The hard work started in the middle of January, when we began giving the ewes some concentrated food each day as well as silage and whatever grazing they could find. Phil mixes his own concentrated 'rations', shoving in about four parts of rolled barley to one part of soya beans, or some other high-protein feed. In January, the ewes were getting about a quarter of a pound a day each, and this works up to a pound and a half or even two pounds just before lambing.

It's a costly business, doling out three or four hundredweight of meal a day, but the raddle colours we used last autumn help. We can tell, you see, which ewes are due to lamb at the end of February and which are due at the end of March and we can make sure the late lambers don't get more concentrates than they deserve.

Some farmers, like Brian Aldridge, keep their ewes indoors all winter, which saves them treading up the grass and eating it bare, and also makes shepherding much easier. Other farmers keep them outdoors right through. At Brookfield, it's a compromise. A few days before lambing's due to start Phil and Jethro bring the ewes down to the Cow Pasture near the buildings, where they can keep an eye on them. Then everybody sets to work rigging up one of the barns and any other spare buildings for lambing. Go to Brookfield on a wet day in mid-February and the odds are that you'll find Jethro and Neil busy with hurdles and straw bales making pens.

Lambing is due to start on 25 February, and, as the date approaches, we aim to get the early-lambing ewes under cover each night. Then, the first ewe gives birth and the fun begins. . . .

In theory, it *could* all happen without any trouble at all. Nature, when all's said, never intended sheep to need human help when giving birth. All we *ought* to have to do is bed the ewes down in a sheltered spot with clean water and plenty of grub and let them get on with it. The trouble is, of course, that Nature never expected every ewe to give birth to two healthy lambs (which is what we aim for) and you wouldn't naturally get 300 ewes congregating in the same place to give birth over a relatively short space of time.

No, the old weatherbeaten shepherd on my calendar belongs, I'm afraid, to some romantic poetical vision of lambing, not to the reality you'll find on any farm today.

Take what happened at Brookfield one night last season. Phil was officially 'on-duty' at the lambing shed, but he slipped down to The Bull for a quick pint and found Tom and me playing cribbage. 'Come on, you can spare ten minutes,' I said, knowing that crib is one game Phil really enjoys. He hesitated, then sat down for a three-handed game. 'I mustn't be long,' he said, 'there's a couple of ewes not far off.' Anyway, the first game was such a close-run thing, with Tom telling Phil he'd forgotten to score one for his nob earlier on otherwise he might have won, that we just had to have a second game. That meant it was ten o'clock before Phil looked at his watch and said, 'Goodness, I've got to get back!'

Outside, as he opened the car door, he said, 'Coming, dad?' with a grin on his face, because he knows how fond I am of sheep, and as you can guess, I didn't need asking twice. I suppose we both thought we'd spend half an hour or so with the sheep, making sure they were all right, before having a glass of whisky for a nightcap and me going off to bed in the spare room.

It didn't turn out like that, though. We knew, when we turned into the yard, that something was wrong because of the noise coming from the barn. 'You go over there while I get some leggings on,' said Phil, hurrying off towards the house.

Inside the barn I found five ewes crying out in distress and, as far as I could make out, six lambs, one of them dead. Twenty other ewes in the pen were milling about in agitation, getting in the way. The noise was deafening.

It took an hour or so of struggling, shouting and the odd bit of swearing to get things sorted out, with Phil doing all the work and me offering advice – not all of it welcome! – from the sidelines.

In the end this was how it turned out. One ewe had twins and was put in an individual pen. She took to them and there didn't seem to be any problem. A second ewe had twins but didn't seem interested in one of them – the second twin would certainly have died if the ewe had lambed outdoors that night. A third ewe had twins, but one of them had died. If Phil had been there when she was born, instead of playing cribbage, she might have lived. But there was no way of telling, and you can't be there all the time. A fourth ewe had started lambing. The lamb's head was showing but its forelegs were bent back. Phil had to lubricate his hand, gently push the head back and find the legs, then help the ewe to lamb. She had a huge single.

It was ewe number five that was the real troublemaker. She hadn't lambed but she was near to it and, as so often happened, she *thought* she had lambed and had 'adopted' another lamb, which meant that Phil and I had got our sums wrong to begin with! She was put in a pen by herself and left to get on with it.

I went over to the house at that point and sat drinking a cup of cocoa with Shula while Phil tidied things up. He had to skin the dead lamb and then fit the skin on to an orphan that had lost its mother earlier in the day, in the hope that the third ewe would accept the live lamb as hers. Then he had to find another lamb and foster it onto the ewe with only one offspring.

The ideal thing, you see, is to send every ewe out with two healthy lambs. We've never achieved it yet, and I don't suppose we ever will. Usually we end up with what we call a 'lamb and three-quarters', or a lambing percentage of 175. But it varies, from season to season, like everything else in farming.

They call it 'February fill-dyke', but it isn't really a wet month, at least not in terms of rain. The dykes and ditches are usually running, but it's often because of melted snow. Rainy days do come, however, and the men have to be found inside jobs to fill their time.

It isn't too difficult on a modern farm, and it's just as well because nobody expects to work outside when it's raining. Neil can always find something to do under cover at Hollowtree, updating his pig records or mucking out a weaner pen. It's the same with Graham; he has half an acre or so covered space for his cows and calves and there are always jobs piling up to occupy a wet day. Jethro can busy himself in the workshop, dodging out when it eases off to take a load of silage and some concentrates up to the sheep. Phil can have a day in the office, trying to teach David something about the paperwork.

When I was David's age, though, there were hardly any buildings to shelter in, and we were expected to work through everything short of a torrential downpour. Many's the day I spent with a heavy sack around my shoulders to keep the worst of the rain off, trimming a hedge with a long-handled hook.

Occasionally, my father would look out of the kitchen door, find he couldn't see Ten Elms Rise because of the falling rain, and decree that it was too wet to work outdoors. (It was amazing, mind you, how often his sharp eyes *could* see Ten Elms Rise when there was something urgent to be done in the fields!)

The first job when we embarked on our 'wet-day routine' was greasing the axles of the carts and wagons. We would lift them up, one corner at a time, on a rudimentary jack, take the wheels off and apply a liberal coating of grease. There must have been enough 'wet days' through the year to keep them properly lubricated, because I never remember a wheel squeaking and I never remember greasing them when it was fine.

When we'd finished we put the tin of grease and the wooden 'spoon' back on the shelf of the tack room and made our way up the granary steps. Everybody knew what was expected of them. By the granary door was a selection of flat sticks about two feet long. Each of us took one, and then we started on the ritual of moving each bag of corn and clubbing to death the rats and mice that appeared. They were mostly mice, and it must have been a comical sight to watch grown men like Josh as well as lads like Ben jumping about like kids, their sticks thumping down all over the place and everybody roaring with laughter. When each bag of grain had been moved and the mice accounted for, one member of the party was detailed to cut pieces of tin and nail them over any new holes to have appeared in the floor since the last 'wet day'. The rest of us sat on the sacks of corn and began darning the holes in the pile of bags that lay over a beam waiting for attention.

To an outsider it would have seemed an odd sight. Two or three grown men and a lad threading their sack needles with binder-twine and darning away, holding up their work for admiration or scorn. It was a time for leg-pulling and story-telling, and talk of the goings on in the neighbourhood. The conversation, and the sacks, usually lasted until the rain was over.

MARCH

MARCH comes in like a lion, so they reckon, and goes out like a lamb, but in my experience the saying is as often as not stood on its head. But then so are most ideas about the weather. I've seen snow in Ambridge in all but three months of the year – July, August, and September – and snowfalls in March are far from being unusual. We were talking about it in The Bull the other night, and Tom was telling us about his wife's cousin from Penny Hassett. She was born in a snowstorm in March, and the midwife only just got through the drifts in time, then she had her twenty-first birthday party in the village hall when outside, there was a foot of snow on the ground, and when she got married, also in March, she had to walk to the church through a blizzard.

It was Josh, back at Brookfield before the First War, who taught me how to read the weather. I remember one afternoon in March, when I was about eighteen. My father had come through the winter badly and now, for the first time any of us could remember, he was kept to his bed with a wracking cough. Since early morning I had been out harrowing the Five Acre. There was a flurry of snow, but I pressed on as best I could because my father's illness had put us behind with the drilling. When I finally got back to the house, dog-tired and aching, to take my boots off and sit at the kitchen table with a mug of hot tea, I found Josh at the kitchen door wanting me to help him take some straw out to the lambs. 'It didn't snow for more than ten minutes!' I protested, but Josh pointed up at Lakey Hill, where the white summit shone in the falling light. 'When snow lies on the hills it beckons for more,' he said solemnly.

It seemed like the daftest thing I'd ever heard, but I had enough sense to trust his judgement. We got a couple of trusses from the barn and trekked off towards the fold. By the time we'd got there the wind had dropped and snow had started falling again, mingling with the blossom on the blackthorn hedge. We put the straw in the lee of the basket hurdles to give the lambs a 'dry lie' and hurried back to the house.

Josh had been proved right, not because 'snow beckons for more' but because he had learned to read his daily weather in the changing light and wind, the clarity or otherwise of the distant hills and in the behaviour of animals and plants. He called the scarlet pimpernel his 'weatherglass' because the flower closed up when rain was coming, and he reckoned that pheasants gave agitated cries of warning hours before thunder was due. Red sky at morning, said Josh, was only a shepherd's warning if the glow crept westward through the clouds. If the redness died within the hour it would be a fine day.

In March, a fine day with a drying wind is what every farmer waits for. Now is the time to get the spring barley in. With a bit of luck, the land ploughed before Christmas will have been nicely frosted and will work down well. 'A peck of March dust is worth a king's ransom' is an old saying that's true enough. If you're out working down the soil and you can see the harrows kick up a bit of dust as they pass, you know you'll get a decent seedbed.

On a clear March day there seems to be a tractor working in every field in Ambridge, preparing the land then getting it drilled and harrowed in, putting fertilizer on grass and cereals and applying chemicals where they're needed. At Home Farm, Brian Aldridge is going all out to get his sugar beet in, although it's often well into April before he's finished.

At Brookfield, Phil will have been out early, down to Lower Parks in the Land-Rover, maybe, rubbing the soil through his hands to see if it's fit to start drilling. Back at

84

Brookfield, he'll have the sense to discuss the matter with Jethro. 'What do you think, Jethro?' he'll say, having already made his mind up, and Jethro, always ready to please, will nod wisely and say, 'We can give it a try, Master Phil,' and he'll trundle off to get the tractor out while Phil has his breakfast. It's not such a happy story an hour or so later, mind you, when Jethro's tractor rumbles back into the yard. 'It's no good, Master Phil,' he says accusingly, as if he'd been against the idea all along, 'the coulters is getting all clogged up. We'll have to leave it.'

Phil stomps off to the office in a temper and he feels even worse later in the day when he sees Brian busy sowing barley with a drill twice the width of his. No farmer likes to see a neighbour's tractors busy when his are confined to the yard, and there's no month in the whole year when this is quite as apparent as it is in March.

A popular chap at this time of year is our NFU secretary in Borchester. He runs the 'lamb bank' and has done ever since the early sixties, when the idea started to catch on. If you have a lamb you can't foster give him a ring and he puts it on his list. If, on the other hand, you need a lamb, he can put you in touch with somebody close by who has one spare.

In early March there will be something like thirty ewes lambing every day at Brookfield and, as I was saying, they won't all be straightforward affairs. Some ewes might have plenty of milk but only a single lamb, in which case we have to try to find another. A ewe might have triplets, and while we usually leave all three lambs on the ewe at first, it sometimes becomes clear that she can't cope with all of them.

You get ewes with one or perhaps two dead lambs, and you get lambs whose mother has died giving birth. Then there's the ewe with a splendid pair of twins but with a mastitis in one quarter, which means she can only feed one of them. Or a ewe whose milk just fails to come, and both she and the lambs are going frantic. It's at times like this that Phil is on the phone urgently to the 'lamb bank', and poor Jill finds herself hauled away from making scones for the W.I. and sent off to Fred Lewis's farm on the other side of Waterley Cross, with instructions to bring back a lamb 'and make sure it's a good strong one!' You need a strong lamb, you see, if you're going to try fostering it onto a ewe who's likely to be pretty hostile at first.

The 'lamb bank' can't always help, and then we end up with something the children always love and Phil absolutely hates: bottle feeding little weakly orphans in cardboard boxes in front of the Aga. Lambs brought up on the bottle are delightful things at first, but they're a terrible nuisance when they eventually rejoin the flock. You see, everything about handling sheep depends on them *behaving* like sheep, so that when you drive them they run. But bottle-fed lambs won't. While the rest of the flock does what it's told, they come walking boldly up to you, hoping you might produce some milk from behind your back. When the sheepdog tries to make them go the right way, they think he's playing a game or just ignore him. They come nuzzling up to your pockets when you don't expect it and make you jump. In general, they make handling a flock extremely difficult and that's why Phil always *tries* to leave a lamb which has to be bottled with its mother, even if she has no milk herself. Once they're domesticated they're ruined, but if the ewe is dead, and the lamb is too weakly for the 'lamb bank', well, there's not much you can do about it – except get the cardboard box out in front of the Aga!

There was one orphan lamb I remember now, even after forty years. It was 1941 or 1942, and I went round the ewes early one morning – we hadn't thought of bringing them indoors to lamb in those days – and found a dead ewe with a dying lamb curled up next to it. The lamb was no bigger than a kitten, and I put it in my pocket to keep it warm while I tended the others. It was so small, in fact, and so quiet that I forgot it was there till I got back into the kitchen and took my coat off. Doris fetched a box with some old rags in and put the wee creature into it. Then she opened the bottom of the stove and pushed the box close to its warmth.

It was then that our Chris came in, ready for school. I can see her now, with her pigtails and wearing a blue mac that did up on the boy's side because it had been passed down from Phil. She looked wide-eyed at the lamb. 'Oh Daddy, isn't he *tiny*!' she said. 'Can I look after him? When I get home from school?'

I agreed, of course, but when she had gone to catch the bus I told Doris that I didn't expect the lamb to be alive by the end of the day. Then a strange thing happened. Jess, the sheepdog bitch, wandered over to the box, sniffed at the lamb and than began licking it vigorously – just as its mother would have done had she been alive. And I swear Jess licked the little lamb back to life. I went out and drew a spot of milk off a ewe that had lambed that morning, and Doris fed him with a fountain-pen filler. He was much too small to take a rubber teat in his mouth.

With a bit of colostrum inside him, the dog's licking and the heat from the stove, he *was* still alive when Chris came running in from school and she took over the feeding. She called him Tiny, and fed him every two hours at first, then every four, then three times a day, and then only twice. That lamb never looked back. He doubled his size in a week and was soon sucking vigorously at a teat on the end of an old lemonade bottle.

Chris worshipped that lamb, and he followed her round like a dog. Jack and Phil renamed our Chris and called her Mary, because everywhere she went the lamb was sure to go.

Then, one day, after it had left droppings all over the kitchen and had been put outside, where it ate all the shoots off Doris's roses, I decided the time had come to keep it in one of the buildings. That was where Chris found it dead one morning when she went out with its bottle. It had got its head stuck in the makeshift hayrack we had rigged up, and hanged itself.

If that had happened to a town-bred girl she would probably have been inconsolable, but death in one form or another is a frequent visitor to a farm, and our Chris soon got over it. She went on to rear a lot more orphan lambs over the years – and Jess, funnily enough, kept up the habit of licking the weaklings, and saved many a creature that would otherwise have died.

'Well, and how *are* you, John?' Colonel Lawson-Hope would say, leaning over the oak table in the livery room at the manor and shaking my father's hand. 'Very well, thank you Squire,' my father would reply, very stiffly. They might very well have met the day before and chatted about the weather or the crops, but on Lady Day, 25 March, they greeted each other very properly because this was when the half-yearly rents were paid, and it was a very formal ceremony indeed.

I was taken along with my father two or three times, and was terribly impressed by the Colonel's coachman, Jenkins, who stood behind him on rent day wearing a top hat with a cockade and bright yellow livery. He was a stern man, and when Walter Gabriel shouted 'Who's a canary?' after him in the village one day he boxed his ears like nobody's business.

There was nothing but smiles, though, for me and Dad when the money was being paid. The agent would read out the amount from his ledger, and my father would haul the money out of a hessian bag and hand it over, and then, because it was the custom, the Squire would give him a half-crown back for luck. After that there would be a glass of sherry and a slice of cake from a side table.

He was a good man, Colonel Lawson-Hope, well liked and respected, and he took the running of his estate seriously. If he thought a farm wasn't being kept up to scratch he'd tell the tenant so and in a fairly *brisk* sort of language too, but if a man had any complaints he would listen carefully and promise remedies.

Every tenant could speak out freely – and that wasn't the case on every estate in those days. Some landowners laid down hard conditions before they would renew a tenancy, calling for a strict form of rotation for crops, and requiring the tenant to let the hedges grow up – to make the partridge rise on shooting days. One landowner at Waterley Cross insisted on his tenant farmers walking a couple of foxhound puppies every year and Lord Netherbourne's father used to demand that his tenants' sons should join the Yeomanry. Very fine they looked, too, riding to Hollerton barracks on a Sunday morning, wearing their scarlet uniform.

In 1914 they changed into khaki and went to war, and so did Colonel Lawson-Hope. The formality and 'pomp' of rent days was over, and it never returned. When I was a tenant I just paid the money to the agent, and although he always asked me how I was, he never gave me sherry or cake and he never had a canary-coloured coachman standing behind him.

Another traditional March event that has changed over the years is the farm sale. They still happen, of course, because Lady Day and Michaelmas are the usual times for tenancies to be handed over. But they're not the *event* they were when I was young – why, as often as not nowadays they don't even have a beer tent!

In those days, though, the entire neighbourhood would turn out to enjoy themselves. They'd roll up in dog carts and traps, and on bicycles and horses, and treat it all more like Stow Fair than the sale of some poor widow woman's possessions.

On the farm, the implements and machinery would be laid out in rows, tools that went back to the Ark, half the time. In the stables the horses would be groomed and would have straw plaited into their tails. There'd be a farm lad standing by to give each beast a 'character'. You wouldn't believe how marvellous those horses were, according to their lads' descriptions. If horses had really been as prodigiously strong as they reckoned, nobody would have bothered inventing the tractor.

The horses, of course, attracted that rare breed of men, the *horse-dealers*. They always struck us simple country-folk as a foxy lot, with their sharp faces and greasy hats, and their gypsy names like Smith and Loveridge. You can see them still, of course, though more rotund and a sight better dressed, at Cheltenham on Gold Cup Day.

They were a decent enough lot, though. I only fell out with them once and that was over Doris. We were at Marfurlong Farm sale in 1932 and Mr Jarman, who was selling up, had agreed to let us put our pony into the sale with his livestock. When the time came, Doris led our pony out into the improvised ring, with our Jack sitting on its back in his Norfolk jacket, and Doris herself done up in her red and white checked dress with a ruffly collar, and scarlet cheeks because she wasn't used to being in the public eye. I was standing behind half a dozen dealers watching. The dealers made comments, of course, and suddenly, to my horror, I realized that the 'pretty young filly with the legs' wasn't our pony at all – it wasn't a filly for one thing, and it was nine if it was a day. They were actually talking about Doris!

Well I was very impetuous in those days, and I seized hold of the chap's collar and rattled his bones a bit and gave him some advice about washing his mouth out with disinfectant, and he and his mates lost interest in the horse auctions and hurried off towards the beer tent as fast as their legs would carry them.

As a result, I'm afraid our pony fetched a very poor price indeed. When I told Doris why, she said, 'Oh Daniel, you daft beggar,' and had the grace to blush a deeper scarlet than she had in the ring.

After the horse auctions would come the sale of the

farm implements. A decent plough, perhaps, a hay wagon, and one or two other things that would fetch a good price, right down to job lots of old iron that went for a shilling. I once saw an early tractor called the 'Overtime' go for £10, while the owner complained bitterly how it had cost him £375 new in 1916. It was a twenty-four horsepower job that used paraffin for fuel and was supposed to be able to plough an acre in an hour. I wish I had that tractor now. It would be worth a pretty penny to one of these 'Farm Museums' that are springing up all over the place.

The cows would be sold next. We'd all go to the cowsheds where the beasts would be in their stalls with their milk records displayed (if it was a good, soundly run farm) and prize-cards stuck over the stalls. If the farmer had any 'notable' cows their names would be written up – but it wouldn't be the names they were actually known by, like Kicker, or Flier, Fillpail or Dairymaid. No, when the farmer was trying to impress, his cows would have names like Aramathea the Third, to indicate a sort of prize pedigree – no matter if the selfsame cow would respond to 'Oi there, old Carrots' at milking time. Old Carrots was a name always given to cows with particularly big ugly teats.

It was a cautious, cunning business was the buying and selling of livestock, and I've no reason to suppose it's changed. If a chap could get rid of a kicker he would stand and lie himself blue in the face about it being the gentlest animal ever born. Walter Gabriel always said his worst bargain was a cow he bought off the rector of Penny Hassett. 'A sweet little Jersey house-cow' was how the rector advertised it, but according to Walter it was the devil on four legs with the wickedest temper he'd ever come across, excepting, of course, his wife Nellie.

Buyers were always suspicious. During one sale – Meadow Farm, I think it was, the Parsons gave up – I came across Joe Grundy's dad in the byre. He had a piece of wood tied to one leg with binder twine and had crouched down next to a cow called Sweet Buttercup. He was trying this cow's four quarters, you see, to find out if she was an easy milker. After a minute there was a thud as the cow kicked out at Fred Grundy's wood-covered leg, and over Grundy went onto his back screaming blue murder. His leg wasn't hurt, but he fell over a pail and sprained his back.

He tried to get compensation from Widow Parsons, and badgered her for months until a few blokes had a word with him in The Bull one night, and told him to leave the poor woman alone. We all knew, you see, that Fred had treated the cow as roughly as he could to test her temperament – and it was only fair that he should pay the price for his mischief.

After the milking cows would come the sale of the dry cows and then the 'followers' – that is the in-calf heifers, the yearlings and calves. The sheep would come next, then the pigs in their sties and, finally, a pathetic little pile of stuff – Mrs Parson's odd sticks of furniture she no longer required and her old farmyard hens.

After the sale, there would be the saddest sight of all, and one you don't come across nowadays, thank goodness, Before the days of cattle transporters and motor lorries, everything had to be moved 'on the hoof', and after the sale was over, and the beer tent was closed, it wasn't just Mrs Parsons but also the animals that had to leave their home, and you would see them plodding along the lanes to their new abodes.

I hadn't been up to Hollowtree for sometime, so when young Neil Carter asked me if I wanted to see his weaner 'bungalows' I jumped at the chance. I'm afraid I still think of Neil as the apprentice, the city lad who didn't know one crop from another when he came to us and once cut a field of oats in mistake for grass. But he's been at Brookfield over ten years now, and he's turned into a very confident chap indeed, particularly when you see him down at Hollowtree, which he runs pretty well by himself. He needs to know what he's doing because the pigs have an annual turnover of around £80,000, which is worth more than we get from either the milk, cereals, or lambs, even if the profit margins don't always match up.

Neil's first job, when we got down there, was to give his pigs some grub. They only had to hear his car door slam to set up the most almighty row, and it wasn't until he'd been round with the feed barrow that we could hear ourselves speak.

While he was getting on with it, I was casting an eye round the unit, which is a mixture of old and new. The dry sows, that's those that are in-pig, are housed in the old buildings of what used to be Jess Allard's farm before we bought it in 1962; the fattening houses and farrowing quarters have all been put up since.

It's basically a sixty-sow herd, which is neither big nor small these days, and all the piglets are fattened for bacon. Across the yard, I could see the 'bungalows' Neil had invited me to look at.

Last year, we switched over from weaning piglets when they were five weeks' old to weaning them when they were three weeks' old. If the sow had any choice in the matter she would go on suckling them for eight weeks or more, but the economics of pig farming, or in other words, the price folk are prepared to pay for their bacon, means we have to get the sow back in-pig as soon as we can. It's a production line, with sows farrowing and baconers going off to the abbatoir every week of the year.

'We aim to get every sow giving two and a quarter litters a year,' Neil told me, his eyes shining with enthusiasm, 'and we like to average eleven piglets a litter – though we're only managing ten at the moment.'

He really loves his pigs, does Neil, and reckons they're the most intelligent and sensitive animals you can find. He used to go to the pictures with Shula sometimes, and she said he was always on about his pigs, and how like humans he thought they were. I've always preferred the sheep, myself, on Lakey Hill, and breeding more or less as Nature intended, even if they are thought to be silly animals!

Neil showed me his weaner 'bungalows'. They are a bank of well-insulated huts on legs, complete with runs. The three-week-old weaners are put into them in bunches of about thirty and thinned into batches of twenty after a couple of weeks. They stay there until they're about ten weeks' old, and weighing sixty to seventy pounds. Then they go into the fattening pens.

Neil likes to 'batch farrow', which means having several sows giving birth at the same time. If one sow has fifteen piglets and another one seven he can even up the litters, and because sows are kept in a sort of cage device to stop them rolling over and crushing their young, they are in no position to object when 'alien offspring' start suckling away at their teats.

It sounds artificial, as if we're mucking about with Nature, and so we are to an extent. Even so, there are few pleasanter sights than a contented sow suckling a good litter, even in the unnatural surroundings of a modern farrowing house!

Sows can be pretty nasty, mind you, and I often think of a story Jethro told us, when we were having our mugs of tea one day.

It concerned a farmworker who knew nothing about pigs, but was told by his boss to keep an eye on a sow as she farrowed. That was what he did. As each little pig was born it scrambled up the side of the sow, looking for the teats –and was promptly eaten up by the sow. (That's what I mean about nasty habits – it does happen from time to time.) Anyway, the farmer returned just as the tenth piglet was being born and scrambling up its mother's side, and the farmworker turned to him and said, innocently: 'Look boss, there he comes again. That's the tenth time he's been round!'

Mind you, it took Jethro a good deal longer to tell the

story, by the time he'd laughed in anticipation at the end of every sentence.

Before I left Hollowtree, I had to look at the three boars, including Neil's pride and joy, Playboy III, and I had to admire the dry sows in their yard, and last but not least, the fattening house, where David had stuck a card up on the wall with a bit of verse on it.

> The pig, if I am not mistaken,
> Supplies us sausage, ham and bacon.
> Let others say his heart is big—
> I call it stupid of the pig.

Neil doesn't approve though. 'They're nothing to joke about,' he said, 'aren't pigs.' And I had to agree with him. After looking round his efficient pig unit, I couldn't help wondering how we had ever *managed* to breed a litter of pigs in the old days, but I can remember the old sows nosing their way round the yard with eleven or twelve healthy piglets in tow. They didn't lie on them, or try to eat them and the piglets grew up quite happily without iron injections and infra-red lamps. I didn't tell Neil what I was thinking, though. Hollowtree is a perfect 'pig palace' as far as he is concerned.

The elm trees running down from Cuckoo Covert used to be smoky-red with blossoms at this time of year, and as you walked Long Field, inspecting the growing corn, you would hear the harsh cawing and complaining of the rooks nesting high in the branches. The elms died and were felled three or four years ago now and the rooks, I notice, have moved down to the beech trees at Foxholes. They're still shouting at each other though, the male rooks perched on twigs by the nests, leaning over now and again to give the sitting female something to eat and then shouting aggressively to the rook on the next branch. The rook has a peculiar face, with no feathers on it, which makes it look rather sinister, and I saw a real ragamuffin the other day. He had drifted down from the trees and landed on a sheep's back, where he was quietly picking away for ticks. I noticed that his backside was almost completely bare and one wing had half of its feathers missing. Presumably they had been blown out by gunshot; it was a wonder the bird could manage to fly at all.

One thing you still see in Long Field in March is the sight of hares playing in the young winter wheat. 'Mad as a March hare' is an old saying, and they do their best to live up to their reputation. To my mind it's one of the happiest sights the countryside can afford, watching them race round in circles, jump in the air, leap over each other's backs and sit up on their haunches to box with each other. I had a puppy once, an unbroken collie, who saw four or five hares in Long Field and ran over to investigate. A moment later he had joined in their fun, chasing round in a circle while another hare chased after him. Hares are beautiful and intelligent creatures, as different from rabbits as red squirrels are from grey, and I believe they make very rewarding pets. There was a vicar in Ambridge once, so the story goes, who had a hare which used to sit up on his knee and nuzzle his ear and would drum his back legs on the carpet when he wanted to be taken out for a walk.

It's a sign, though, that spring is really here, when you get a bright, sunny March afternoon, and the hares throw caution to the wind as they dance their delightful mating ritual in Long Field.

APRIL

ON Lady Day 1919 I took over the tenancy of Weston Farm and became a farmer in my own right. I went back to look at it not long ago. It's just a couple of fields now, with most of the old hedges grubbed out, and the farmhouse is used by Brian Aldridge as a store for old machinery. The gable wall's had a hole punched in it so that vehicles can be driven under cover, and when I poked my head inside the kitchen I found an ancient green Fordson tractor sitting where I used to eat my supper. Empty oil cans and rolls of wire netting were piled against the fireplace, where I used to sit smoking a pipe after my day's work.

Outside, though, the small copse behind the house is still standing, and blubells and anemonies cover the ground thickly, just as they did sixty-odd years ago, when I rode over from Brookfield to 'take possession' – an independent lad of twenty-two, out to make his way in the world.

I'd been released from the army two years before, in the spring of 1917, when my father was taken into hospital with tuberculosis, or consumption as it was called then. Frank was seventeen and eager to learn, but he wasn't experienced enough to run the farm, and old Josh, wise through he was about the weather and a hundred other things beside, was lost unless somebody told him what to do each morning. Our other chap had joined up back in February. The war was nearly over, he said, and he didn't want to be left out of it completely. My first job when I got home was to apply to the War Agriculture Committee in Borchester for a replacement,

97

and they sent me along to the post office to fill in a form. Eventually, they sent along a young baker called Terence, whose chest was nearly as weak as Dad's, and who had been found unfit for military service. He could have stayed in the bakery, he said, but the biscuit flour was irritating his asthma. Funnily enough Terence turned out to be one of the best workers we ever had at Brookfield. He was paid 25s. a week, and we had to give him 2s. 6d. a week 'subsistence' – but I could claim the half-crown back if I filled out another Ministry form once a month. It was the first subsidy I ever claimed from the government, but in a lifetime of farming it was far from being the last!

On Sunday afternoons, Mother, Frank and I would drive over in the trap to visit Dad. Once when Ben was home on leave from the 9th Battalion King's Own Shropshire Light Infantry, he came to the hospital with us and that's the last time I can remember the entire family being together, that Sunday in the convalescence ward, with everybody laughing because Dad was well on the road to recovery, and Frank making cheeky jokes about Ben's moustache, and being clipped round the ear, and the ward sister complimenting Mum on the three fine sons she had.

'Fine sons?' said Mother, 'I'd trade them all for a daughter.' She'd always wanted a daughter, had Mother. During the war she didn't go round the village collecting for the Red Cross, or the troops' comforts fund, but for something called the 'Schoolgirls of the Empire War Tribute'.

Ben went back to his regiment and Frank was called up and went away the following June. After the war, Ben only came back to Brookfield once before he emigrated to Canada and we had a terrible fight over Doris, in the small paddock behind the house. He would keep calling her 'M'oiselle' and trying to pat her bottom, you see, and then one night he tried something he shouldn't have tried, even if she had been a French girl.

He thought he was tough, but I was nearly two years older than he was and I licked him.

Still, that was in 1920, and I'm getting ahead of myself. In the summer of 1918, my father was firmly back in charge of things at Brookfield and there wasn't really room for me except at busy times. It's very irksome, you see, even with the best will in the world, to be *told* what to do after you've been the boss for a few months. And my father did have a trick of saying, 'Never, you mind lad, just do it,' if ever I queried something. Anyway, the Squire's agent, Mr Forsyth, must have realized how impatient I was, and he must have thought I'd handled Brookfield well enough while Father was ill, because he tapped me on the shoulder one day. Would I be interested, he said, in taking over the tenancy of Weston Farm next Lady Day? He didn't have to wait long for an answer!

Weston Farm. I've told you what it's like now, and there are two pen-and-ink drawings on the sitting-room wall at Glebe Cottage, done by an artist who rented a room in the village one summer. The first shows the farmhouse, with ivy growing up the front and Doris sitting on a chair in the doorway shelling peas. The other picture is a scene behind the copse, with the farmhouse chimney showing through the trees, and me ploughing behind the best pair of horses I've ever known.

In more matter-of-fact-terms, Weston Farm was forty-one acres, or seventeen hectares as some would have it these days, which makes it sounds even smaller, and it had a reasonable set of buildings, including a small dairy, and some useful grass. The house wasn't much better than a worker's cottage, but being a bachelor at the time, I wasn't particularly worried. The tenant, Charlie Moss, had been killed the year before by a Shorthorn bull, and his widow had decided to get out.

I had nearly £400 saved, a lot of it put together in the eight or nine months since I'd been offered the tenancy. I don't think I'd taken a single day off work during that time. I went in for everything, from hedging to shearing, from rabbit catching to hay trussing, and I borrowed the horse and wagon from Brookfield to do a spot of haulage. I took on anything that paid, and because farm labour was terribly scarce by 1918, and farmers were doing very well in the wartime boom (the price of wheat had more than doubled since 1914), I found that many things paid very well indeed.

Mrs Moss had got eight cows, a couple of pigs and some poultry. At the sale I bought five of the best-looking cows, which took most of my money, together with a plough, harrows, a chaffcutter and a turnip slicer. And that was it. I couldn't afford the pigs or the poultry, and anyway I was worried they might tie me to the place too much. 'There'll be time enough to think about poultry,' I told my mother, 'when I'm a married man.'

'And when will that be, then?' she asked, crossly, because she was fairly longing to have a daughter-in-law. 'I haven't time for girls, Mother,' I replied, 'not with a farm to run.' Neither of us could guess that I'd get to know a certain girl in a couple of months' time and change my mind about everything!

In the meantime, I was learning to live on my own. My parents lent me a bed, an old table and a couple of chairs, and my mother packed enough jam and chutney to keep me going for six months. On my last morning at Brookfield we'd finished breakfast and Dad said, 'Well go on, put Prince in the old cart and get him round to the door. We'd best take your stuff over there, and you with it.' I got the cart, and loaded my things onto it, then Dad went and harnessed Bessie and hitched her up behind. 'What do you want the mare for?' I remember asking, and the reply came, as irritating as ever, 'Never you mind, lad!' At that moment I was really glad to be leaving home!

When we'd driven over to Weston Farm, though, and unloaded, he turned to me and said, 'Well, you've got a pair of horses and a cart, so you'd best get to work. I'll walk back to Brookfield.'

Well, I'd been relying on borrowing Prince and Bessie from time to time, but to get them as a gift was something I hadn't dreamed of. They were my favourite horses, and what was more Bessie was in foal and likely to deliver the goods in a month's time. The gift represented a fair sum of lost profit, because Prince would have been sold into the town that year for a good price, and Bessie would have gone on breeding. I felt very grateful.

The rent for Weston Farm was 38s. an acre, or about £80 a year. That's less than our Phil pays for half a ton of dairy nuts today, but as I stood in the yard the next morning after milking my little herd, I was blessed if I could see how to pay it.

Then I had a bright idea. I would grow three acres of potatoes and sell them in Hollerton – in my mind I was already driving a cartload to market and getting a good price for them.

I chose one of the fields furthest from the buildings and began marking it out. After a few minutes I heard a shout from the yard, and looking back saw Dick Allard, Jess's cousin, waving to me. He had two horses and a cart with a single-furrow plough in it. 'Come to plough you in,' he said, grinning, when I went back to see what he wanted.

'Ploughing-in' is a custom that has long since died out, but in those days it was common for friends and neighbours to come along and do half a day's ploughing to help a new chap get a start. And the folk of Ambridge rallied round me, that morning. By the time Dick and I had opened up a couple of furrows apiece, we were joined by two others. By milking time, the field was glistening brown all over.

It was too early to plant potatoes, of course, but by the third week of April, I had worked the field down to a beautiful mould. I borrowed a ridging plough and hired a lad out of the village and between us we got those three acres planted by hand and covered up. We were just in time, too, because on the 27th and 28th we had nearly a foot of snow. I was cursing my bad luck, because I had to keep the cows in the yard and open a rick of hay I'd taken to – there was no chance of them finding any grass – but I reckon that snow did me a power of good as far as spuds were concerned. May and June were hot and dry that year, and I believe it was the melting snow that got my crop off to a good start.

We had a nice bit of rain in August to bulk the tubers out, and I lifted a good crop the following month. Dad came over after he'd finished the Brookfield harvest, and gave me a hand in return for my help with his corn.

So there I was, launched as a farmer – and with enough money to pay the first half-year's rent at Michaelmas.

I planted my potatoes by hand, with the help of a village lad, but Phil belongs to a small farmers' co-operative that shares modern machinery and storage. Some time towards the end of April it's Phil's turn for the potato planter, and I like to go up to Brookfield and watch them at it for an hour or two.

It's always good to lean over a gate with the sun on you're back while somebody else does the work and I especially enjoy spud planting because it brings a few strangers onto the farm, and reminds me of the days gone by, when there was much more 'gang work' on farms. Not that we have a very big team of visitors, it's generally just the tractor driver and four 'girls' who sit on the machine feeding the potatoes into the planter. But those girls do manage to bring a bit of life to the place!

They're always laughing and singing, or else swearing and shouting, and they don't think a day's been well spent unless they've made Jethro angry and made Neil blush. The 'innuendo' in some of their jokes is quite extraordinary, and you ought to see poor Neil's expression as the double meaning sinks in. Jethro never learns. 'I'd give you girls what for if I had the chance!' he shouts at them, 'my eye I would!' – and they hoot with laughter and tell him to meet them behind the bus shelter after closing time.

At dinnertime they eat their sandwiches in the workshop, giggling and whispering on one side of the stove while Jethro sits and glowers on the other. Neil often finds he has a sow at Hollowtree that he 'must nip down and look at'.

People don't really change much. There's a nice lass, Rosie, who's been coming with the 'gang' for three or four years now, and she always reminds me of another Rosie who came to Brookfield with some land girls during the last war. They were a mixed lot, those girls, and there were some pretty colourful characters among them.

They were billeted in a hostel out on the Felpersham road, and you could hire a gang of them by the day. We learned, by experience, that the bigger the gang the more trouble you were likely to have! On one occasion, we needed some stone-picking done on a field we had ploughed up as a part of the war effort. I was on the Agricultural Executive Committee – or War-Ag as it was known – and I felt I had to set an example. Anyway, we had ten land girls delivered to us one cold April morning, and by nine o'clock there were signs of unrest. By eleven o'clock, several of them had knocked off – they hadn't joined the Women's Land Army to do convicts' work, their spokesman told me. How, she asked, was picking up my stones going to help beat Hitler?

I tried to explain that the stones would damage the potatoes later on, and they agreed, reluctantly, to go back to work. But at dinner-time four or five of them took off and walked back to the hostel and a couple more disappeared during the afternoon. There were only three of them left working by the time the lorry turned up to take them home.

A friend of mine on the War-Ag found himself in a

very strange situation. He was going round the farm one morning when he heard a cry coming from a ditch. Thinking it was a new-born lamb he leaped off his horse and went to investigate. It wasn't a ewe that had given birth, though, but one of the land girls. She was a buxom wench called Maisie, who had often worked for us at Brookfield. I don't think they ever discovered who the father was, but Maisie took her young son back to Manchester, and the other land girls steadied up for a time.

The girls didn't only work in gangs, of course, a lot of farmers had them working full time on the holding. At Brookfield we had a nice middle-class girl from Oxford called Ruth and I don't think she had ever set foot on a farm before, except out hiking. She came in May, when we were busy castrating and tailing the lambs, and she looked awfully smart in corduroy breeches, Aertex shirt and a green tie. Doris brought her out to the sheep pens, and I said, 'Hello, Ruth,' and she said, 'Hello, Mr Archer,' and took one look at what we were doing and fainted.

She soon recovered, though, and became a willing, if not always useful, member of the team. She once harnessed one of the horses with the bit beneath his chin instead of in his mouth, and wondered why he didn't respond to the reins. On another occasion she stooked five acres of beans upside down (mind you, it's not always easy to tell one end of a sheaf from the other with field beans). But the moment I'll never forget was the day she came past one of the pens just as a calf was being born. She had no idea what was happening, or what Simon and I were doing there, or why the cow was bellowing and moving round in agitation. Then the calf was born and, as it slowly slipped out of the back end of the cow, Ruth exclaimed: 'Good Heavens! When on earth did she swallow that?'

Ruth eventually left to go and work for a market gardener in the south west. That was in April 1943, just after the government had restarted the special trains that brought cut flowers up from Cornwall and the Scilly Isles. They'd been stopped as an economy measure, but there was such an outcry that the Ministry of Transport had to start them up again. It always struck me as a marvellous thing that folk could make so much fuss, at a time like that, over a few daffodils.

Anyway, I've got very affectionate memories of those gangs of land girls, of Ruth and Shirley, the girl who followed her and stayed at Brookfield for nearly two years. I like to pop up and watch when they're putting the spuds in now, and listen to the girls singing and joking up there on the planter.

This may be the last year I'll see them, though. Phil and his farmers' group are talking about buying an automatic planter for next year. It'll be efficient, I dare say, and do the job in half the time, or at half the cost, and Brian's computer will say it's a wonderful investment. But it won't do anything to cheer up an old man like me – and I don't suppose it'll ever make Neil blush!

'When you can cover five daisies with one foot, then it's time to be thinking of putting the cows out.' That was my father's advice to me and I daresay it was *his* father's to him, so it must have been guiding us Archers for more than a hundred years.

I passed the tip on to young David the other day, when he was talking of turning out the herd. He just threw his head back and laughed. 'It depends on what size shoes you take,' he said, when he'd recovered, 'doesn't it, Grandad?'

Well, they might have more scientific ways of deciding things these days, but I usually do a cross-check on my lawn at Glebe Cottage, and it's amazing how often the old saying fits. Mind you, I couldn't really expect David to take advice involving *daisies*. They don't encourage daisies these days you see. Or buttercups. If they see too many of them in a field they think it's time to spray it or plough it up.

But there's truth in most old farmers' observations, and there does seem to be something about the growth of daisies that tells you a bit about the soil temperature and generally how Mother Nature is getting on with the job of ushering in another spring.

When to open your yard gate and let the cows out is a decision you let the cows themselves take part in. Just as in October they *know* it's time to be indoors and will stand around looking at the grass instead of eating it, well in the spring they *know* when they ought to be let out and they'll follow you down to the gate expectantly, instead of going back into the sheds.

What they don't know, of course, are the other considerations Phil and David and Graham are taking into account. Is there enough grass to keep the cows going permanently, or will it be used up in a week? Spring grass is a marvellous tonic for dairy cows, which is why it's sometimes known as 'Dr Green', and it can boost the milk yield by ten per cent or so, but if you run out of grass and have to bring them back in again the yield drops back and you don't get another boost when you turn them out again.

Another thing you have to consider is the amount of fodder you have left in store. Sometimes you are forced to let the cows out early because you're running out of silage or you might keep them in a few extra days to finish off the silage left at the back of the clamp.

The day they were finally let out was always a big occasion at Brookfield. It meant the end of six months' hard slog cleaning the yards every day, mucking out the sheds and cleaning dirty udders. For the cows it meant fresh air and freedom, and didn't they appreciate it! Doris used to love watching them as they tried their first grass after the winter, and I can remember our Phil when he was three or four years old, swinging on a field gate and clapping his hands as the cows galloped round kicking their legs in the air. 'More!' shouted Phil, 'more, more!'

I didn't want them to do any more, I can tell you. They weigh more than half a ton apiece, dairy cows, and I could hardly bear to watch in case one of them slipped and broke a leg. Phil has the anxiety now and he lets them out in dribs and drabs. At milking time, he leaves the yard gate open so the cows can go into the field eight at a time as they leave the parlour, their empty udders slapping from side to side and as soon as they see the green pasture ahead break into an ungainly trot.

After half an hour or so they settle down quietly to graze, and about three milkings later you begin to see the results in the yield. Not long after that, as the grass works through their systems and loosens them up, you get your first dung-laden tail swishing across your face as you labour in the parlour and you wonder if letting them out was a good idea after all!

I was in Martha's buying a few sweets for my great-granddaughter Kate, and as Martha stood on her little steps to reach the bottle of mint humbugs (an indulgence of my own, Kate has a preference for chocolate buttons) I suddenly thought of Miss Crook, who owned the village shop when I was little, and of being brought in one day by an aunt who bought me a halfpenny-worth of acid drops twisted up in a three-cornered bag.

I must have been four at the time, because it was the year Queen Victoria died, and Miss Crook had a coloured print on the wall of the Queen's funeral cortège leaving Windsor. I was standing with an acid drop in my mouth, looking up at it and admiring the long columns of scarlet-coated guards wearing bearskins and others wearing shiny brass helmets with plumes of white feathers in them. On the way back to Brookfield I puzzled my poor aunt, demanding to know *why* God had allowed the Queen to die when she was such a good

107

Queen, and then one of the pram wheels came off and we had to persuade a reluctant Ben to walk the half-mile back to the farm.

It was Martha climbing her little steps, though, that made me think of Miss Crook, because as soon as we children were old enough for devilment (when we were five, say, and had started school) we used to plague her something terrible. One trick was for one of us to go in and ask for a farthing's-worth of aniseed balls. She kept them on the top shelf, and had to get out her steps, unfold them, climb up and get the jar, climb down, weigh them out, then climb up and put the jar back, before folding her steps away. A few minutes later, Walter would go in. 'A farthing's-worth of aniseed balls, if you please, Miss Crook,' he'd say. And a few minutes later it would be Sam Blower's turn, and after him Silas Winter.

I don't know why we thought it was so funny to tease her, because she was a gentle soul and if she didn't smile much she never lost her temper, unlike old 'Art', who lived in a little tin-roofed shack up behind Hollowtree. Art was the roadman before Zebedee Tring and there was always a pile of loose chippings next to his hut. Every time we kids went past, and it was surprising how often we found we *had* to go past – it was the work of a moment to grab a handful of chippings and fling them onto his roof. The effect was always dramatic. A roar of rage from Art and us disappearing down the road as fast as we could. On one occasion, though, we flung the stones, turned to run – and found Art standing behind us! He missed Ben but grabbed me and gave me a few hearty thwacks with a hazel switch. I could hardly sit down that night, but I didn't dare let on to my father or mother, or I'd have been given another beating.

A sense of humour, mind you, is a peculiar thing. I've got one, of sorts, and so has Shula. But animals don't have one, and neither does our Phil.

Doris and I were staying at Brookfield one night, a few years back, 'baby-sitting' while Phil and Jill were out at the South Borset Hunt Ball. Doris went off to bed and I was left up playing draughts with Shula, who was about twelve at the time. I tried to make her go to bed of course, but she was a strong-willed girl, and she wouldn't go till we'd thought of an April Fool's trick to play on her mum and dad. Eventually we did, and off to bed we went.

Next morning we were both up at six. I think I'd have forgotten our little 'joke', but Shula was there tapping on my door and out we went to the farrowing house, where Shula chalked APRIL FOOL in large letters. Then I went back to the house and woke Phil up. 'Quick!' I shouted, 'the gilt's started farrowing. She's got out of her crate and smashed the lamp – *and* the water!'

Phil staggered out of the bedroom, grabbed an old mac over his pyjamas, squeezed his bare feet into his gumboots and raced out past me and across the yard. About six feet from the farrowing house he saw the message. Then Shula appeared giggling and I came out behind roaring with laughter.

Phil didn't laugh though. He gave us both a withering look, muttered, 'I suppose you think that's funny,' and walked back to the house with as much dignity as a man with a hangover in a mac, pyjamas and gumboots could manage.

Not a great sense of humour, you see. Mind you, as he told us icily over breakfast, he *had* been out checking the gilt at a quarter past four that morning, when he and Jill got back from the Hunt Ball, and he knew she couldn't be farrowing really.

You could only work that sort of trick on a stockman. Ring Brian Aldridge at six o'clock in the morning to tell him there are aphids on his wheat and he'll probably reply: 'Really? I expect they'll still be there at ten o'clock,' before turning over and going back to sleep.

It's a simple sort of thing, a country sense of humour. Childlike according to some, I daresay. But it's always been the same. Take the occasion, back in the twenties, when Tommy Reed and one or two others decided to have a 'race' to Hollerton Fruit and Vegetable Market. Times were very bad for farming after the 'war boom' was over, and the smaller farmers round Ambridge were growing all sorts of what you might call 'opportunist' crops – turnips, swedes, cabbages, sprouts – anything they could think of which could be sold for immediate cash.

Anyway, in The Bull one night, Tommy, George Grundy, Sam Blower and one or two others decided that next morning they would start from their farms at four o'clock and see who could get to market first. They put five bob apiece into a hat as prize money, and went on with their game of dominoes.

After a bit Tommy, who had the smallholding where Carol Tregorran has her nursery nowadays, said he felt tired and slipped off home. The others looked at each other, then carried on with their game. But when they left the pub at closing time one of them said, 'Let's go home past Tommy's.' And there outside his yard, was his dray loaded high with sacks and crates, ready for a smart getaway the following morning.

There was no evidence that Tommy intended *leaving* before the agreed time, but the others decided they ought to make quite sure. So they quietly unloaded the dray, then lifted it bodily over a low wall and set it down in a small yard which had a gate too narrow for the dray to get through. Then they quietly loaded it up again.

It was a bit unkind, perhaps, but it provided laughs in bar parlours round the neighbourhood for weeks. And Tommy was never what you'd call the most popular of people.

When I was a boy I was sent to the village shop for a 'penn'orth of pigeon's milk', but that was an old country joke. It was Walter Gabriel who came up with a new one. We had a vicar who was terribly proud of his lawn in those days, and spent most of his time mowing it or rolling it or keeping it free from moss and daisies. Well,

Walter took against the chap for some reason. Something to do with the vicar clouting him round the ear at Sunday School when he fell asleep during 'Onward Christian Soldiers'. Next morning, which was cold and frosty, Walter crept out and shovelled up a dozen frozen molehills from one of our fields. Then he laid them carefully on the vicarage lawn. The vicar was round at Ricky Nobbs the molecatcher's by nine o'clock, but Ricky never managed to catch anything, even though the vicar made him try for a week and use every method under the sun.

MAY

LAKEY HILL on a fine May morning, with a gentle breeze blowing from the south west, and the old hawthorn hedge weighed down with early blossom. Can there be a better spot? I haven't travelled widely, but I can't imagine anywhere in the world I'd rather be. I was up there with Phil yesterday, helping him look over a bunch of heifers David thought were showing signs of an eye infection called 'New Forest Disease' that can blind them if it's left untreated. I say I was 'helping', but nowadays that means Phil going round inspecting the animals while I prop up the front of the Land-Rover, soaking up the sun. It had been raining earlier and the air was crystal clear, giving me a wonderful view over Brookfield land and right across the vale to the distant Malvern Hills.

It's no wonder so much has been written about May. It really is a marvellous month. Poets go on about lads and lassies falling in love, but a farmer could wax lyrical about the land itself. It's the time of year when everything is growing and you can almost watch it happen – the crops, the livestock, the grass. I'd been up on Lakey Hill ten minutes and could have sworn the green bracken shoots breaking through the ground all round me had sprouted half an inch while I was there. Well, a quarter of an inch, anyway!

Over to the west I could see David spraying the winter barley in Long Field against weeds, his bright red tractor disappearing every now and again behind the pale green foliage of Cuckoo Covert. In fact, I could *smell* him spraying, you can't mistake that slightly sweet, sickly pong of hormone weedkiller. Beyond Long Field I could just see the cows strip-grazing behind the electric fence in Trefoil, across the road from the farm buildings. I couldn't actually see the electric fence, at such a distance, but what else would be keeping all those little black and white specks huddled up into one end of the field?

I couldn't see Neil, either, but a feedstuff lorry was backed into the yard at Hollowtree and no doubt he was behind it, somewhere, helping the chap unload.

Looking the other way, towards Willow Farm, Jethro was going round the ewes and lambs in Paradise and Blacklands. They've got them split into two lots to make handling easier, and talk about growing – why, those lambs seem to have doubled in size every time I see them. Phil was talking of sending some off for slaughter in a week or so, which sounds very early to me. It seems only yesterday they were lambing, but farmers these days expect to start sending them off at ten or eleven weeks. It's not much of a life for them when you think about it!

Below us, in Ashfield, I could see the potatoes showing through nicely, and over the hedge was one of the fields of grass put up for silage. David seems to have taken over the grassland management – with Phil's willing consent I might add – and he was murmuring the other day about starting on silage about the 22nd of the month.

Beyond the grass was as nice a crop of winter wheat as I've ever seen at this time of year in Skipperley. We can only hope for plenty of rain later this month to help it along – but only at *night*, of course, so it can't interfere with our other work!

Over the River Am I could see the Five Acre, which still retains its old name although it's actually seventeen acres nowadays. We planted spring barley there about five weeks ago and it's coming along well. David says the winter-sown barley is already coming into ear, which I find pretty astonishing. But it is getting earlier and earlier. They always used to say that May shouldn't go out till the wheat ear has come in, but I haven't always found wheat in ear in May myself. Perhaps I haven't looked hard enough.

Across the valley, one of Brian's chaps was busy spraying sugar beet on a stretch of ground bordered on two sides by huge splashes of yellow. That's the oilseed rape, a crop that was pretty well unknown in England when I was farming. Back in 1970 there were about 10,000 acres being grown – I remember because Phil was going on about it as the 'coming thing', and I was telling him how coming things have come and gone a dozen times in my lifetime, and how we ought to stick to what we knew best.

Anyway, oilseed rape has become such a popular crop in this country that we're heading for *half a million* acres now and this year, Phil's having a go at Brookfield.

It's a member of the cabbage family, but it isn't grown for fodder, as you might expect, but for its tiny black seeds, which are crushed to produce oil for margarine and all sorts of other things. As a crop, I have to admit that it has tremendous advantages for the farmer. Brian called it a 'godsend' when he was round advising Phil about it the other day. Not only is the price supported by the EEC at a fairly high level, but it can be drilled and harvested with the same equipment we use for cereals. To make it even more worthwhile, rape provides a very useful 'break crop' by preventing some of the diseases you can get if you plant corn over and over again on the same land.

It has also certainly brightened the May landscape! All down the vale yesterday I could see swatches of chrome yellow on field, hill and headland, stretching far into the distance, and I was reminded of the days before farmers used herbicides on such a scale. You would see meadows dazzlingly bright with buttercups at this time of year. Midsummer Meadow, at Brookfield, was famous for cowslips. There was one spring, just after Jack was born, when Doris brought him out there one afternoon and, while I sat drinking my tea and playing with him, she picked a huge bunch of flowers. There were more cowslips than blades of grass in that meadow, and she could fill her basket without stretching more than an arm's length. Jack was crawling off through the cowslips on the other side of his rug, trying to find a corncrake that was making its strident 'craak! craak!' as it ran hidden through the grass.

It was a very *unremarkable* sort of afternoon, a mum and her little lad playing in the meadow for an hour. But it couldn't happen like that now. Cowslips are so rare they're almost a protected species, and I haven't heard a corncrake for the past twenty years. They've both been a victim of modern farming methods.

Phil finished inspecting the heifers and we went down to Paradise, to see if Jethro needed any help with the sheep. He hadn't found any sign of New Forest Disease, just a couple of animals with watery eyes that would need watching. Perhaps they'd been gazing too much at the vivid yellow rape as the sun poured down on it across the valley!

Stow Fair day is on 12 May and it's also Old May Day, when we used to have a maypole in the village. It wasn't the usual sort of maypole, mind you, but a sort of tower made out of twigs and covered with leaves and there would be a chap inside it who could move its arms about. They called it a 'Jack in the Green' at Heybury. All the schoolchildren used to get the day off. There would be dancing on the green and tea and buns. I have no idea when it died out, sometime in the early twenties I imagine. Doris always reckoned that the first time she spoke to me was on Old May Day, 1911, when she came to Brookfield pushing her brother Tom in his pram. She was being sent round the farms by the Sunday School teacher, asking for ribbons and stuff to deck out the 'Jack in the Green'. Tom was whimpering and whining (so Doris said) and I poked him with a stick and called him a little stoat and that made her cry. I've never been able to remember the incident myself but Doris said I was nasty to her because she was the keeper's daughter, and she had a wonderful memory did Doris.

115

It is also traditional in these parts to plant kidney beans on 12 May. A lot of folk put them in earlier, of course, but there's always the danger of frost until the end of the month, and frost is something a tender young kidney bean plant can't stand. Sammy Whipple's dad was a ploughman at Home Farm, and he knew an old rhyme about the planting of corn and kidney beans.

When the elmen leaf is as big as a mouse's ear
Then to sow barley never fear.
When the elmen leaf is as big as an ox's eye
Then says I, 'Hie, boys! Hie!'
When elm leaves are as big as a shilling
Plant kidney beans, if to plant 'em you're willing.
When elm leaves are as big as a penny
You must plant beans if you mean to have any.

I was telling the rhyme to Mr Fletcher the other night, when I ran into him in The Bull. He's taking up gardening this year, and was waiting for Joe Grundy to bring him some special 'kidney-bean fertilizer'. He's also on the committee of the Cricket Club, and he had one of the old club record books with him. 'I was going to bring it along to the cottage and show you,' he said. 'There's an account of how your brother Ben scored 68 not out when he was only thirteen years old.'

I knew all about the game, of course. It was between the single men and the married men and one of the farmers was declared 'out' when his top hat blew off and onto the wicket, dislodging the bails. Ben's score was a record for several years. It was a terrible job to get runs on a village pitch in those days. Outfields were unmown and the wickets were rolled once in the spring and that was it. If you did run up a score, well, the other side's umpire would do his damnedest to get you out, because umpires were a partisan lot and as cunning as you like. For many years the Ambridge umpire was Walter's dad, old Nelson Gabriel. He was a very big man you see, being the blacksmith, and

116

that was useful when he made a contrary decision. Once the vicar remonstrated with him about 'playing the game', and 'honest English sport' and Nelson went red in the face and bawled, 'I've been umpire for five years, and I've umpired this side to the top of the league!'

The game I recall best was an away match against Penny Hassett when I was about eighteen. It was remarkable because when we set out from Ambridge there were only seven of us, and we couldn't think how we were going to manage to play. Two of our chaps were in camp with the volunteers, Tom Whipple our 'miracle bowler' had broken his arm back in February, and another bloke was ill. Anyway, we got to Traitor's Ford and there was George Grundy waiting for us, so we gave him a rousing cheer and on we all went. At Penny Hassett the vicar told his coachman he'd have to play, even though the poor chap had never played cricket in his life. Then Rosemary and Polly Wynyard turned up to watch their brother, and in desperation, the vicar bundled Rosemary into the wagonette and told her to change into a pair of flannels and a blazer. I can't think how we got away with it. She was bowled for a duck, but she stayed in long enough for Ben to make a dozen runs. Women's cricket is common now, of course, but it wasn't the thing in those days – at least not in Ambridge!

I was telling Mr Fletcher all about it when Joe Grundy came in carrying a sack over his shoulder.

'Here you are,' he said, putting it down next to Mr Fletcher's chair. 'Don't let Sid Perks see it, he's been nagging me to get him some of this for weeks.'

'I'm very grateful, Joe,' said Mr Fletcher, opening the top of the sack and looking inside. 'Pooh!' he said, 'what a smell.'

'That's the trace elements,' said Joe. 'That's what does your kidney beans a power of good. That and the minerals and the dung. You'll have bean plants climbing up round the top of your chimney by the end of July, mark my word.'

'And it's pure new wool, you say?' Mr Fletcher went on.

'That's right,' said Joe, giving me a hard look, 'pure new wool steeped in special manure. Can I get you a pint, Dan?'

'Well,' said Mr Fletcher, 'it seems very good value for five pounds.'

'Yes Joe!' I said. 'You *can* get me a pint!'

What he was selling Mr Fletcher was a sackful of dags – the bits of filthy wool that have to be cut away from the sheep's backsides when we're getting them ready for shearing. Joe must have begged them off Jethro, I suppose, or one of Brian's workers. At any rate, he was quite right about their being good for kidney beans. I always shove some dags in the bottom of the trench in my garden.

'It's been a very satisfactory evening,' said Mr Fletcher, beaming at us. 'Mr Archer's told me a poem about when to plant my beans, and you've given me something to plant them in. I suppose that's what village life is all about.'

'I could have told you a poem,' said Joe. 'He who bathes in May, will soon be laid in clay. You won't catch me having a bath before June the 1st, I can tell you.'

Unfortunately, Joe made his last remark rather loudly, and Sid heard him and came over complaining about the smell. 'You have a bath or you're banned,' he said, much to Joe's indignation, 'it stinks worse than a sheep pen in here.'

> 'The vly, the vly, the vly be on the termutt
> And 'tis all my eye for me to try
> To keep vly off the termutt!'

Many is the time I have heard Tom Forrest sing the above, and joined enthusiastically along with everybody else in the familiar chorus. But the 'fly' was no laughing matter when I was younger, whether it was on the turnip, swede,

118

kale or cabbage. One of my very earliest memories is of my father, slumped in despair in his kitchen rocking-chair, telling us that the fly had destroyed the turnip crop at Brookfield. That was May 1901, a bad year for the fly, I think, as we weren't the only ones to suffer. I can picture the scene now – Father looking old with worry, although he was only in his early forties, Mother in her long skirts wiping the flour from her hands after rolling pastry, and Ben playing with a puppy on the floor. It is so vivid in my mind because of what happened next. 'Sunday or no Sunday,' said my father, getting wearily to his feet, 'I'm going up to drill them again.'

That was when I realized, young as I was, what a terrible thing had happened. Nobody did field work on the Sabbath in those days, and there was many a farmer who would stand and watch a hay crop spoil rather than risk offending the Almighty. I asked Father if I could help, not that a lad of four and a half could do much, and I was rewarded by being given a little bag of turnip seed to carry. I felt very proud as I followed Dad out of the door!

Nowadays you buy seed ready dressed against fly, or 'flea beetle' to give it its proper name, but there were no chemical cures in my father's day. The beetle came suddenly and worked quickly, almost as soon as the seedlings appeared, and if you forgot to go up the field for a couple of days your turnips could have come and gone. It wasn't at all unusual to have to sow twice, sometimes three times, before you got a crop through the danger stage.

There were various things you could do to try and save the plants. Some farmers used to spray paraffin to deter the pests and later on, when slag became common as a fertilizer, we used to walk up and down the rows shaking the stuff onto the tiny plants, using an old sack with the corners cut off. Slag didn't poison the beetles, but it coated the plant leaves in dust and made them a bit less palatable to the hungry insects. A chap from Aberdeen, who had come south to be a farm manager at Loxley, had taught me the trick of using slag. Trust the Scots to know how to protect their 'neeps'.

Slag itself was thought of as something of a wonder fertilizer when it was first used on the phosphate-starved soil round Ambridge, especially on grassland. But some regarded it with deep suspicion. 'It won't make bad land good,' said Joe Blower, 'but it will make it *look* good.' Joe was a very old-fashioned fellow who believed in honest manure and nothing else. The best fertilizer in the world, he maintained, was the contents of the Ambridge privies.

I don't know what Joe would say about the stuff we put on the land these days. In my lifetime, four things have happened to revolutionize farming: mechanization, plant breeding, livestock breeding and the development of 'agro-chemicals' – and, for sheer ingenuity, the chemists take a lot of beating.

From being pretty well powerless to deal with the 'vly', which was the situation in my father's day, we now have a chemical for just about every insect, weed or disease you can name. The boffins have gone way beyond killing charlock in wheat, which I thought was a miracle when we tried it during the last war. Now the chemical firms can sell you something to kill couch, chickweed, blackgrass, wild oats, docks – and some sprays are so clever they get to work before the weeds even start showing. Today's farmers depend on chemicals so much that some, like Brian Aldridge, leave permanent tracks through their corn so they can get onto the land whenever they like. They call them 'tramlines' and they allow the tractor and spayer or fertilizer spinner to treat the crop without damaging it.

Brian puts his 'tramlines' down when he's drilling, but Phil doesn't. He thinks that if you make 'tramlines' to start with, you'll be tempted to use them and go in with some expensive spray or other when you might well have been able to do without. But if something does need treatment he's quite happy to move into a standing crop with a sprayer and trample his 'tramlines' down as he goes along. Although he always hopes for a trouble-free crop, I notice that most of his winter-sown cereals end up with wheelmarks through them.

Our first attempt at chemical control at Brookfield, dealing with charlock during the last war, was very primitive by today's standards, a bit like comparing the bow and arrow with one of these Exocet missiles. But the bow and arrow worked, in its day, and so did the sulphuric acid we sprayed on Trefoil in 1943. I couldn't differentiate between the corn and the thistles because of their hormonal make up, the way modern sprays do. It worked simply because it landed on the flat leaves of the charlock and burned them, and ran off the upright leaves of the wheat leaving it unharmed.

I would love to have a photograph of us, as we were on that May morning in the early forties, preparing for action. We'd borrowed a sprayer from the War-Ag – a huge monster with what looked like an outsized beer barrel for a tank – and everyone had been told to parade in their oldest clothers, smear their faces and hands with grease, and wear goggles. What a sight we must have been!

What we were scared of was that part of the operation involved diluting the concentrated sulphuric acid – or 'oil of vitriol' as they called it – which didn't sound quite so dangerous.

Well, we got the job done without injuring anybody, which was a miracle looking back, and we sprayed eight acres in Trefoil, a field which runs alongside the road. To be honest, I was keen to try spraying because I was so ashamed of folk seeing the crop as it was – you couldn't see the wheat for the charlock over most of it.

I don't think that any pesticide we've used since – and we've had some pretty dramatic responses from some of them – surprised me as much as that acid did. It worked a treat. The charlock simply shrivelled up and the wheat grew up through it. We harvested well over a ton to the acre, which was quite good in those days, especially as the

121

wheat price had more than trebled since the outbreak of war.

That early experience with agricultural chemicals had a strange sequel though. A week or two later we were in the yard at Brookfield and Stan, one of my chaps (who wasn't very bright), said, 'Mr Archer, my trousers be a- rotting. Look you here.' And he pulled at the material of one of his legs, which came apart in a little rent. 'Let me have a go,' said Peter, the youngest who was working for me while he waited to be called up, and he grabbed poor Stan's trouser leg and gave it a sharp tug. To the surprise of all of us, the entire leg came away revealing Stan's long johns. He was so upset I had to fetch him an old pair of my trousers from the house.

It didn't take long to work out what had happened. He must have splashed his trousers, somehow, when we were filling the tank with acid. I told Doris about it later, and she said what a sensible fellow Stan was. 'What, getting splashed with sulphuric acid?' I asked, astonished. 'No, keeping his long johns on,' said Doris. And she recited the old saying, 'If you would the doctor pay, leave your flannels off in May.'

I said nothing, but I thought we were lucky not to have had to call the doctor for something more serious than a chill.

Well, for 'agro-chemicals' that was only the beginning. We've had forty years of development by the scientists, and the whole landscape has been altered. Gone are the thistles I spent so many days labouriously spudding out of the growing corn before the hormone weedkillers 'MCPA' and its brothers came along. Gone are the poppies which stained the cornfields red; you hardly see them now, except on the occasional verge. And gone is the charlock which ruined many a wheat crop, and so often sent me tired to my bed after hours of slashing the weed-tops as they rose above the corn.

We wasted years of time and effort on weeds and diseases that now disappear with one pass of the sprayer, but I can't help wondering if we aren't depending on chemicals a bit too much these days. I might be an old-fashioned stick-in-the-mud, but I look at Brian up at Home Farm and at our Phil with David keeping him 'up to date', and I sometimes think they've become hitched to a sort of chemical treadmill and can't get off it. They spend enormous sums of money 'just in case' – and believe me, there *are* enormous sums of money involved these days. I reckon if Brian read all the literature pouring through his letter box, and listened to all the reps knocking on his door, he'd have a tractor and sprayer chugging up his tramlines every day of the week.

At Brookfield we still stick to a rotation of sorts, but a lot of farmers now don't bother with anything as outmoded as that. They defy Nature, as it were, and rely on sprays and fertilizers to get them out of trouble. But Nature doesn't like being put to odds – at least not in the long run – and in my view, a wise farmer is one who uses chemicals as an aid to sound farming, not as a replacement for it.

I still possess seven of my father's old account books, records from the 1880s and 1890s, showing how Brookfield prospered in the years before I was born. They're grubby and yellow with age and the ink has faded in a few places, but I like to sit by the fire when I've had my dinner and puzzle over them, fitting together the jigsaw of my father's life. He never talked about it much, you see, or perhaps I never thought to ask. He died when I was twenty-eight.

Will Phil go through my record books one day I wonder? He certainly isn't bothered at the moment. But neither was I at his age – I was far too busy making the current year's accounts balance to worry about what happened in the 1880s.

It's fascinating to read them now, though. I came across an agreement from 1888 the other day – that was two years before my father took over Brookfield on the death of *his* father - and it concerned the sale of thirty acres of grass keep at Meadow Farm. The agreement was in my father's own copperplate handwriting, and he must have copied it down after the sale to make sure he had all the details correct. It reads:

LOT 2 30 acres grass keep. £15   5s. 0d.
Agreement
Be it remembered that the sale by auction this 31st day of March 1888, I, John Archer, was declared the purchaser of Lot 2 at the price of £15   5s. 0d. and I have paid into the hands of the vendor's agent the sum of £1   10s. 6d. by way of deposit and in part payment of my purchase money and I do hereby agree to pay the Vendor at the times and by the instalments mentioned in the second condition the sum of £13 14s.   6d. being the remainder of my purchase money and in all respects to fulfil the foregoing conditions of sale and I, John Archer, do hereby confirm the same.

Purchase money	£15 5s. 0d
Deposit	£ 1 10s.6d
	£13 14s 6d

1st July First moiety	£ 6 17s 3d
29th September Second moiety	£ 6 17s 3d
	£13 14s 3d

This agreement shows that my father, as a young man, was involved in a spot of 'private enterprise' on his own account, just as I was thirty years later and our Phil thirty years after that! My father had probably been keeping some ewes and lambs, and my grandfather must have insisted that he find his own keep for them during the summer. He wasn't supposed to be a very sympathetic chap, wasn't my grandfather, Daniel William Archer. We still have a photograph of him, taken in about 1860, with his top hat set at a rakish angle and a devil-may-care look on his face.

The most interesting thing about the agreement, though, is the rent paid for the grass keep, about 10s. an acre. This year the going rate for summer grazing round Ambridge was around £80 an acre. I know the grass is a lot better now than it was a hundred years ago, and I know that farming in the 1880s was going through a depression, but even so 50p to £80 takes a bit of explaining.

What's happened, of course – apart from ordinary inflation – has been the amazing rise in the value of land itself. I bought the original Brookfield, as a sitting tenant, for £50 an acre back in 1954. It's now worth more than £2000 an acre, and if Brookfield, including the livestock and machinery, was put on the market it would make well over £1,000,000 – even after the bank overdraft and mortgage were paid off.

It's pretty astonishing really. Particularly when you think of my father going to that sale of grass keep a hundred years ago, with the two sovereigns to pay the deposit tied up in his handkerchief.

JUNE

WHEN I walked down to school on a June morning, just after the turn of the century, a familiar sound was that of metal set against the huge grindstone in the smithy yard, where the men of the village were sharpening their scythes against the hay harvest. And when Phil walked down to school at this time of year he must have listened to the clatter of the horse-drawn mower coming from fields on every side.

The hay harvest is still with us, I'm pleased to say, but it has been joined on a pretty massive scale by the 'silage harvest'. Not that silage is a particularly new idea. Most folk think it's been invented since the last war, but in fact it was known in my grandfather's day. My father's copy of Frean's *Elements of Agriculture* had four or five pages on silage – or 'ensilage' as it was known then. We didn't try it though, and it was Joe Blower, sometime in the 1920s, who first had a bash in Ambridge. He made it in a sunken cart track, and topped it with a layer of soil, and it didn't bear any resemblance at all to the huge clamps you see nowadays, with their black polythene sheeting kept down with old tyres. The principle was the same though. 'I'm just pickling the grass in its own juices,' said Joe, when he invited me round to inspect the stuff. Pickled it might have been, but it smelled awful, and I didn't dare try it at Brookfield. We had just started milk retailing at that time, and I was afraid that silage might taint the milk and lose us customers. It seemed a lot of work, as well. Getting the chopped grass into the clamp, then covering it over, and then having to dig it out again to feed to the stock.

There's no denying that cows thrive on the stuff when it's well made, and you are nothing like as dependent on the weather as you are with haymaking. All it needed was modern machinery to make it popular, and nowadays it's joined all those other products on the farm that are 'untouched by hand'.

So I can see why Phil and David are so keen on it. The grass is piled up in a heap in the summer, and the cows pull it out for themselves during the winter. They'll say there's more to it than that, of course – cutting at the right time, wilting, consolidating, sealing – but it's the simplicity of the operation that really appeals. What I don't like is the *bustle* it involves. Neil tearing round with the mower, David going hell-for-leather with the forage harvester, Jethro and Graham to-ing and fro-ing with trailers at top speed, and Phil busy with a tractor and buckrake back at the clamp. None of them has time even to give you a wave, let alone stop for a chat. Give me haymaking, any day!

Mind you, haymaking is pretty well mechanized now. The real difference, I suppose, lies in the end product. One is sweet-scented and a pleasure to handle, and the other is soggy and foul-smelling. That's a generalization, of course. I've known hay so poor that when you lifted a forkful you were enveloped in dust (the sort that gave Joe Grundy his 'farmer's lung') and I've seen silage so wholesome it tempted you to try a mouthful.

We cut the hay with scythes when I was a lad, and the worst haymaking disaster I remember at Brookfield was in 1910, which was the year I left school, and the year when my father bought a grass mower. He wasn't really happy about it at the time, partly because he thought the scythe did less damage to the growing grass – it didn't crush the stems where it cut them – and partly because a labourer and his scythe were very cheap to hire. A man would work for fifty hours a week for 14s. in 1910, so why spend £20 on a mower? But he grudgingly gave in to progress, and bought a second-hand mower, and almost at once landed us in trouble.

The grass mower, you see, made things just that little bit too easy. When the men were using scythes they were never tempted to cut too much at one go. Five blokes could mow a five-acre field between breakfast and suppertime. And they wouldn't move on to mow another field, except during a very dry spell, until the one they'd just finished had been put up into 'cocks' and made safe against the likelihood of rain.

But once my father got out there, with two horses harnessed to that second-hand mower, well, common sense seemed to desert him. It was the power of *machinery*, you see, when you've been used to earning things by sweat of your brow – the sheer joy of sitting up there and watching the fingers slide through the grass and the blade move to and fro. Before he knew it Father had cut an entire six-acre field, and the next day he moved on into the seven acres next to it, and by late afternoon we had thirteen acres of hay lying cut.

A few days later the rain started. Some of the hay had been turned and some had not. There were seven of us out there working with forks and rakes; Mother, Ben, Frank and me, as well as Father and our two regular workers, but we just could not cope. Hardly had the sun come out, to make us think we were getting somewhere, than we would get half a day's rain. And so it kept on, never giving us a chance. It was a heavy crop, to make matters worse, and needed a good deal of making.

In the end, we carried about four acres of it, in poor condition, and the rest was carted off and burned. We couldn't leave it to rot in the field or it would have killed the grass beneath. Fortunately we had a rick of hay in hand from the previous season, and that saw us through, but it took a couple of seasons before we got straight again, and for the rest of his life Father regarded the temptations of machinery as infinitely more terrible than the temptations of strong drink – and that's saying something, when you think how the 'Temperance Movement' was sweeping through the countryside in those days. It must have been 1910 or 1911 that a famous preacher came to Ambridge, invited by the Methodists, and when he'd finished his sermon half the men of the village walked behind him to the bridge, and threw their pipes into the river, and promised never to give way to alcohol or tobacco ever again. Some of them kept it up, as well. One of the Wynyard cousins never drank another drop between then and his death in 1937.

Mechanization came to Brookfield, slowly, over the years. Between the wars we were using a mower, a rake, a tedder, a 'sweep' (first pulled by horses and later pushed by an old motor car) and a swathe turner. We were still stacking hay loose until the beginning of the fifties, so most of my working life was spent haymaking the hard way. I used to think myself a pretty dab hand at building a rick with loose hay, mind you, although the first time I tried it with the 'new-fangled' bales, I ended up with a red face. The stack looked fine when we went to bed, but when I went out to milk the next morning, it had collapsed and bales were scattered all over the yard. That was when I decided to invest in a bigger Dutch barn – at least when you're stacking the hay in one of those you've got something to hold the corners in.

I was reminded of those pre-baler days when I wandered into the workshop at Brookfield, and found a row brewing between Jethro and 'Master David', as he will insist on calling him!

'You can't destroy that, Master David!' Jethro was saying, his voice full of indignation, 'You never knows when we might need it and then where would we be?'

'Oh, for Heaven's sake, Jethro,' David was saying, a very irritated look on his face, 'when could we possible need it again?'

'Well there's no saying, is there? There's no saying at all.'

The thing they were talking about was an iron rod, about eight feet long, pointed at one end and with a ring at the other David, it seemed, wanted to cut it up and use it in a welding job he was doing. Jethro was scandalized.

'Twenty years!' he said. 'That's how long it's been hanging on that hook to my certain knowledge. That's a fact, ain't it, boss?'

I had to admit the rod had been hanging on the workshop wall for more than thirty years, ever since we went over to hay bales. It was a rick rod, and its purpose was to test the temperature inside a rack of loose hay.

We were so vulnerable to the weather, you see, before all this machinery came along to help us, and there was always the temptation, if it looked like raining, to cart the hay while it was still on the green side, and hope it would cure in the rick. Usually it did, but sometimes it caught fire instead. If we were worried we would push in a rick rod, and pull it out from time to time to see how hot it was. When you could not hold the end in your bare hands you began to get worried. If it was even hotter the next time, you considered cutting open the rick to let it cool off. Sometimes you left it too late, and it actually caught fire inside the rick.

I remember my father opening a smouldering rick when I was a little lad. He was taking it apart very carefully, hoping desperately that the air would cool the heated, smoking hay, and not ignite it. I came up thinking what fun it was, grabbed a forkful of the charred hay, and tried to stir it into flames by blowing it. The next thing I knew I was lying on my back on the cobblestones, my head reeling from the blow my father had given me. 'Are you trying to burn us all to death?' he shouted. I can't blame him, looking back. He must have been worried sick, because that rick represented months of winter fodder.

I was telling all this to Jethro and David, and Jethro kept nodding his head saying, 'That's right boss,' and after a bit David went off to find another bit of rod to do his welding with. 'All right, I give in,' he said, and I had to feel pleased – although he was quite right, I don't suppose we'll ever need to use a rick rod at Brookfield again.

A lot of hay used to be stacked in the field where it was made, and in winter it would be cut with a hay knife, a long, sharp blade about two feet long with a handle, and tied up into trusses that weighed about a half-hundredweight each. It was a pleasant enough job, to take the horse and cart and truss enough hay to keep you going for a few days, while the old horse browsed the side of the rick. But it gave the biggest fright of his life to 'Bony' Grating, a chap who worked for Jess Allard back in the early thirties.

Jess had the next farm to Brookfield in those days, and I was busy laying a hedge at the top of The Croft one morning when I heard my name being called, and saw 'Bony' Grating running towards me down the lane. Bony never looked healthy at the best of times – tall, and as thin as a heron he was – and on that dank, misty winter's morning he looked like a storybook ghost as he waved his arms and shouted, 'Come quickly! There's a hand in the hay!'

Well, I went back with him to the rick in Jess's Long Field and there sure enough, lying on the ground, was a human hand. It had fallen out of a truss of hay as Bony chucked it onto the wagon.

Jess, it seemed, was at Borchester Market for the day, so I told Bony to stay with the horse while I went for the police. Then I raced across The Croft, scrambled over the Am on a fallen willow, and ran across what is now Cow Pasture, but in those days was three separate fields. I managed to saddle the cob without Doris seeing me – I didn't fancy having to explain about severed limbs lying around in a field next to ours – and galloped off to the village. I must have looked a bit like a character out of a 'wild west' film as I cantered past the green and up to the police station, where P C Bates was pottering around his garden.

He wouldn't believe me at first, and asked me if I was drunk, but I wasn't known for being a madcap, so in the end he put on his tunic and cape and followed me back to

Jess's place on his bicycle. When we got there, poor Bony was in a worse state than ever, stroking the old mare and staring, hypnotized, at the hand as it lay on the grass.

The affair caused quite a stir, and was written up in the *Borchester Echo* and the Felpersham papers, and the police were all over the place until they'd managed to identify the body which was found in the rick. It wasn't murder, though. The explanation accepted by the inquest was simple but very, very horrible.

A tramp, it seemed, had chosen to sleep on the rick while it was being built. The next morning the gang had arrived and as often happened, had started the elevator and begun pitching hay onto it while the rick builders were still climbing the ladder. By the time they arrived at the top the tramp, probably still befuddled with cider from the night before, was covered with loose hay. He was literally built into the rick and died from suffocation. If Bony had continued cutting hay he would have revealed the man's head and shoulders.

Thank goodness he didn't. Bony never recovered from seeing that hand and he kept having nightmares about it for years afterwards, or so he said.

The ricks of loose hay have long gone. Haymaking at Brookfield is now so mechanized that it's almost a one-man operation. Phil hasn't gone in for the big round bales, like Brian, but the conventional bales are easily handled from the seat of a tractor. Now, instead of leaving the hay out for a week or more, I've seen it cut, turned and baled in as little as thirty-six hours.

Watching David bring a loaded trailer in from the fields, I couldn't help smiling, and thinking back to a hay harvest one year between the wars. It was a good harvest, one of the best, and it had taken us just over two weeks, with Doris out there in the fields with us on every day except Wednesday, which was when she made butter. Ned Larkin had just come to Brookfield and I had Simon, of course. Simon was the great expert when it came to hay. 'Reckon we can start carting now in the Five Acre,'

132

I'd say, and he'd say, 'No us can't, the swath be full of fire-leaves and they take a deak of drying.' And we'd leave the Five Acre for another day or two, because I respected Simon's judgment almost as much as my own.

The weather was close and thundery, the hay seeds clung to our skin, and a multitude of rabbits got caught and killed in the knives. Jack was about ten, and making himself useful, with Phil running round behind him all the time instead of looking after our Chris. In the afternoons Doris brought our jugs of tea, with bread and ham and homemade cakes – goodness knows how she found the time to make them. On the last night, with the final load of hay safely pitched up on the stack, we sat in the kitchen with a stone jug of cider that had been lying cool in the pond all day.

It was a hot, sticky night, with the thunder rolling towards us from the Malverns, and we sat and listened to it with grins on our faces, because the downpour could come now, and welcome; my three ricks were safe under their tarpaulins and filled with grass cut at its sweetest. I remember the sheer *satisfaction* of it all, and the cider pouring into the blue-rimmed mugs, and Ned, who was a forward-looking, inquisitive sort of chap in those days, saying as how he heard that a farmer over Felpersham way was cutting his grass at night.

'He's got them electric lights in all his trees,' said Ned. 'I daresay we'll be doing the same afore long.'

'You're a daft beggar,' said Simon, amazed.

'Then there's another bloke,' Ned went on, 'as cuts his grass afore it comes to flower, More goodness in grass cut young and dried with 'lectricity than any amount of seeded hay, or so he reckons. I daresay we'll all be a-doing it soon.'

'Well it won't happen in my lifetime,' said Simon, quite affronted by the idea, and I agreed with him, as I refilled their mugs.

'No,' I said, 'nor in mine either.'

* * *

The other great job for June, after the silage and the haymaking, is the shearing. The experts will tell you it ought to be done by the end of May, but we nearly always leave it for a week or two. Shearing, you see, is best done when the 'rise' has taken place. That means when the grease has risen in the wool, making it much easier for the shearers to handle, but it doesn't happen until we've had a spell of warm weather. Until about twenty years ago we used to shear the ewes ourselves, but now, like most folk round here, we employ a gang who go from farm to farm.

And do they rattle through them! Of course, they've good reason to work quickly because they're paid at so much per head. There are usually three or four of them in the team, and we might spare somebody to help them, provided we're not in the middle of silage making. Phil's often down there, of course, watching over things but not getting too involved. When Neil and Jethro are roped in they're used to catch the ewes before shearing, and to roll the fleeces afterwards. But it's not a job they look forward to. It's so fast, you see, and *they're* not on piecework like the shearers. 'Get a move on, mate!' the shearers shout, and Jethro gets very red-faced and flustered.

The shearing is done in one of the sheep pens at Marney's, where they spread a tarpaulin to keep the wool clean. I generally wander down for an hour or two, but it's not the place for a quiet chat. What with the ewes and lambs kicking up a fuss at being separated, and the noise from the petrol engine, and the whir of the shears, and all the shouting, you can hardly hear yourself think. Not, as Jethro said the other day, that he particularly wants to when them 'Kiwis' are about. The shearing gangs are often New Zealanders, you see, travelling round the country and picking up a decent bit of money.

I started 'shearing' as a tarboy, at the age of six. In other words I was not doing any shearing at all, but going round with a can of Stockholm tar, and when a shearer shouted 'Tar, boy!' I'd run over and dab a bit on some poor ewe that had been nicked by the shears.

134

This was in the days of hand shearing, and some men were a lot more skilled than others. There was one young chap my father employed who just couldn't get the hang of it, and the poor ewes were being cut all over with the razor-sharp shears. By the time I'd finished with the tar some of them looked like Jennifer's Jacob sheep – black and white all over. I was telling one of our 'Kiwis' about this, a year or two back, and he said if I was doing the same job on some New Zealand farms today I'd need a needle and thread instead of a tarpot. They work at such a speed, he said, that the ewes can be badly wounded if a shearer's hand slips.

The best part about shearing in the old days, and it didn't change much before the last war, was washing the sheep first. Nobby Styles had the disused mill on the Am, just this side of the village, and he used to pen the water up at shearing time. Then all the farmers around would take their sheep, in turn, to wash them. I think Nobby charged us a halfpenny a head for the privilege, and the 'fun' of the occasion we got for nothing. It was quite a village event, you see, with a lot of splashing and larking about. Nobby had fixed up a board for us to stand on, so we could push the sheep under one at a time, but there was always a lad – one of the Blowers usually – who would get in among them, swimming around and ducking the ewes. He wasn't paid to do it, he was just there for the fun of it. Towards the end of the day, when we had more or less finished, someone was bound to get pushed in the water, and there'd be screaming and laughing, and as often as not we'd all end up having a swim.

There is still a premium for washed wool, but I don't think anybody bothers to do it in this area nowadays. We always reckoned the sheep shore better for it, although you had to leave them a week or so to let the grease get back into the wool.

Like so many routine tasks in farming, shearing was a more leisurely business in those days. By the time we reached the thirties we'd abandoned the hand shears in

135

favour of mechanized clippers on a flexible shaft. These were powered by turning a large wheel – and that was usually the job for the farm 'lad'. He would start off energetically enough in the morning, but by mid-afternoon his energies would flag, and the cutters would begin to die in your hands. 'Come on, boy!' you'd shout, 'put a bit of muscle into it!' – just as if you were encouraging a tired horse. We would manage twenty sheep between milkings, and if it took three or four days – well, what did it matter? Every fleece was carefully stacked in the loft, to be collected and weighed by the wool merchants later on.

We were only a small place, of course. Sammy Whipple can remember being the 'lad' at Home Farm, where they used to have a sort of 'feast' in the farm kitchen when shearing was over. I went to it once, for some reason, and I recall how hot it was in the kitchen, with everybody's clothes covered in grease from the wool – pure lanolin, mind, and very good for the skin – and the flies buzzing about us, and the old stove still hot from boiling up beef and onions. Sammy still knows the little verse his boss used to recite:

> Here's health to the flock,
> May God increase the stock,
> Twenty where there's ten,
> May we all come here,
> Sheep shearing again.

Nowadays at Home Farm, Brian gives his 'Kiwis' a couple of glasses of beer, and they sit outside round his swimming pool.

They wouldn't tolerate me long in today's shearing team. They go through the Brookfield flock in a day and a half, with two of them at it, and they only stay at Brian's for three days, even though he has 600 ewes to clip. The big leap forward in speed took place during the sixties, following a visit to England by a New Zealander called

Godfrey Bowen. His technique of rapid shearing caught on, and most folk practise it now. Mind you, there aren't many who can outshear Mr Bowen – he once got through 559 ewes in a nine-hour day. They were Welsh ewes, though, and only half the size of ours!

When I was a boy Midsummer's Eve was far more important than it is now. There was magic in the air, and witches about, and many a girl believed that if she sat in the church porch at midnight, she would see the form of the man she was going to marry. I don't know of any local girl who ever tried it, although Rosemary Wynyard said she was going to. That was the year after Polly married Tom Whipple, and Rosemary was feeling very low. It's as well she didn't wait up in the porch, mind you, because she married Piggy Atkins in the end, and Piggy was an ugly fellow. The sight of his 'form' in the churchyard at midnight would have frightened any girl to death.

Farmers had their superstitions too, and believed they could protect their crops from evil spirits by walking round them on Midsummer's Eve carrying flaming torches. It sounds ridiculous now, but the end of June is a very anxious time, with the corn ripening, and just think of the superstitions folk believe in nowadays! Jethro's wife, Lizzie Larkin, wouldn't go into Borchester if her horoscope told her to avoid long journeys.

I never saw crops being 'protected' with burning torches, and by the time I took over Weston Farm in 1919 most of the old customs were changing. We had a bonfire on Lakey Hill, and burned an effigy of a witch, but that was just a bit of fun for the lads and girls.

It's a wonder to me how any of us had the energy after shearing and haymaking, but we kept the custom going for five or six years. It was after the bonfire in 1918 that I started courting Doris. She was working at the Manor House and I daresay she was supposed to be tucked up in bed on Midsummer's Eve, but there she was on Lakey Hill with two other maids, all sharing a mug of cider and laughing away. I can picture her now, standing in the light from the fire, watching the witch burn, and holding a flower in her hand – a sprig of St John's wort. It's a lovely plant, at its best around the midsummer.

Anyway, I made some joke about only daftheads picking flowers in the middle of the night, and she turned pink and the other two girls giggled fit to burst. I only found out afterwards that if a girl plucked a sprig of St John's wort on Midsummer's Eve and kept it in a handkerchief till Christmas, then wore it in her bosom, her future husband would come and take it. That was the story at any rate!

I saw Doris a few times that autumn – once when she was walking back from the Manor to her dad's cottage on a Saturday afternoon, which was her time off, and once, I remember, when I had to take a couple of hurdles up to the Manor for some reason and she was out at the back. We used to banter and joke a bit. She was always the 'keeper's lass' to me, even though she did work at the Manor, and she used to call me the 'farmer's lad' and asked me the price of turnips.

At Christmas, though, we met at a dance in the village hall, and I asked her if she'd still got her St John's wort stuck down her blouse, and she told me not to be cheeky and denied ever having had a sprig in the first place! She was admitting it by the end of the evening, mind, and I was telling her she'd better not let anybody take it off her but me. That was how we got engaged to be married.

Shula and David are always on at me to tell them the story, and now young Elizabeth's started. They seem to think it's the funniest story in the world, but to me, looking back, it seemed a very natural thing to have happened. And even if the St John's wort was a bit scratchy for Doris, it worked, didn't it?

138

JULY

JULY used to be a quiet month at Brookfield. The hay harvest was usually over and the corn harvest was yet to start. The cows were beginning to dry off, ready for the autumn calving, so there was less milking to be done. The lambs were getting fatter day by day, but were nothing like ready for the butcher. All we could harvest were the strawberries in the kitchen garden and we would eat them for tea every day with thick yellow cream. At some point in the month, Doris and I would slip off for a week at the seaside and the chaps would do the same.

How things have changed! And most of it in the last ten or twelve years. Winter barley is the biggest culprit, I suppose. We used to sow barley in the spring and harvest it in August, but now they've brought in high-yielding varieties that can be sown the previous autumn and harvested in the middle of July. It means, of course, that you can utilize your machinery better. When you've only got one combine and a small team, the earlier you can start the corn harvest the better, and in July the days are longer and the dews not so heavy. But Doris wouldn't have been happy. She'd had enough trouble talking me into a week at Aberystwyth as it was, but if we'd been growing winter barley I'd never have gone away.

Then there's the oilseed rape – that's usually harvested in July. And David is busy with his 'second-cut silage', topping up his clamps with more grass or, if he isn't doing that, he's out spraying the potatoes against blight. You may think that the main corn crop can be left alone; it's all in ear now and changing colour rapidly, but no – there's a chemical you can spray on it that will kill the weeds

139

growing in the bottom, so that you have a nice, weed–free stubble ready for the next crop!

As if all that isn't enough, Phil is lambing earlier, so a weekly selection of lambs for the abattoir has to be organized. The price of lamb drops week by week in the summer, so he wants to get them off as soon as they are fit, which means when they reach between eighty and ninety pounds. It's a job Phil likes to do himself, so every week, you'll find him down at the sheep pens with Jethro, drawing out perhaps forty or fifty to go with somebody's mint sauce or redcurrant jelly.

There's one July job that hasn't changed, not since I was a lad or my father was a lad, and that's the sheep dipping. We do it three weeks or so after shearing, because the wool has started to grow a bit by then and can hold enough dip to do some good. I couldn't say how far back sheep dipping goes – 150 years at least; if an advertisement by 'Messrs Thomas Biggs' is to be believed. Phil came across it in a farm catalogue for 1894 that was jammed behind a desk at Brookfield and only came to light recently when he was having a bit of a spring clean.

'Sheep dipping composition for the destruction of tick, lice etc. and for the prevention of fly, scab etc.' says the advert, and goes on: 'This composition has been in successful use for Half-a-Century and Millions of Sheep and Lambs are annually dipped with it. Specific for Scab and Shab, which will be found a certain remedy for eradicating that loathsome and ruinous disorder.'

Messrs Biggs's composition cost 5s. a gallon, which was enough for thirty sheep, or it could be bought in a bottle for 1s. 3d. My father had written 'one gallon ordered' in the margin, so he must have believed in it. The Brookfield flock in 1894, two years before I was born, must have been less than thirty sheep, or he would have needed more.

Dipping is beneficial to sheep in any number of ways. It kills ticks, keds and lice, and it prevents fly strike, but it is the danger of Messrs Biggs's 'loathsome and ruinous' scab that makes dipping a legal requirement. At one time, the village bobby had to be present on dipping days and I can picture P. C. Bates now, with his blue tunic buttoned up to his neck, and the sweat pouring down his face in the hot sunshine. He'd bicycled out to Brookfield, you see, then walked up the field and he wasn't normally a very active man, wasn't P C Bates.

The Ambridge policeman when I was a boy was P C Simmons, a gaunt, grim-faced officer of the law who had, until 1913 at any rate, a large, Germanic moustache. He was the only person who ever terrified my brother Ben – and that happened, curiously enough, because of the sheep dipping.

It must have been 1904 or 1905 when the Ambridge 'Sick and Provident' society was still going strong and still holding its annual club day in the week before St Swithin's. Most villages had sick clubs in those days. For a penny or two a week, labourers and their families were provided with money and food during illness and there was coal given out in November and January. It was the generosity of the Squire and gentry that kept the sick clubs going in hard times.

Anyway, the Ambridge society held its club day in July, and farmers were expected to give their chaps the day off. There was a service in St Stephen's in the morning and after that there was the club dinner. It was a curious business, because the club members didn't sit down together, they queued up outside the bakers and collected a meat pie and raisin pudding for each family, then took them home to eat. We didn't have a village hall then, of course, but the organizers *could* have borrowed a barn off a friendly farmer. Perhaps they all liked eating in their own parlours.

We Archers had nothing to do with the club dinner, of course, but Ben and I were allowed to go down in the afternoon and join in the games on the village green. It was at those games, on a warm afternoon some eighty years ago, that my brother Ben somehow 'acquired' a yellow and red-painted hoop stick. I knew it wasn't *his* stick. It couldn't have been. When we went down to the village after our dinner he was bowling his hoop along with a bit of twig out of the hedgerow, but on the way back he suddenly produced this specially carved piece of wood with a painted handle.

'Where d'you get that from?' I demanded, sternly I expect, as befitted an elder brother.

'Get what from?' replied Ben, concentrating on making his hoop go in marvellous spins round the potholes. He was a demon with his hoop was Ben, forever bowling it at tremendous speed, jumping ahead of it, trying to jump through it and sending it crashing all over the place. Goodness only knows how many times my poor mother had to find a penny so he could get it repaired by Nelson Gabriel at the smithy.

'I've seen Walter's little Alice with a stick like that,' I said. 'How did you get hold of it?'

'Won it in a bet,' said Ben, still dodging about, making his hoop do back-spins and pretending to be unconcerned.

'Won little Alice's hoop stick in a *bet*!' I exclaimed.

'I never said it was her stick.'

'Well it's a girl's stick isn't it? It's meant for a wooden hoop not a metal one – you'll have all that paint off in no time at all.'

Ben gave me a nasty look, then said he'd found the stick in the grass and why didn't I just mind my own stupid business. Well, I waited till we were in bed that night then I had a real go at him. He'd pinched it, I said, stolen it and that meant he would burn in hell fire and no mistake. Ben said he didn't mind, he'd like it. Then I said how little Alice's mother would tell P C Simmons and how we would all be made to stand up, one after another, at school, and how P C Simmons had *ways* of getting the truth out of us and then Ben would go to prison. Ben said nobody could make him say anything, and if they did he'd be better off in prison, because at least I wouldn't be there to annoy him.

Next morning I'd forgotten all about the incident. It was only a bit of wood after all, and little Alice might well have dropped it in the grass. But Ben must have been more scared that he'd let on. Halfway through breakfast there was a knock at the door, and my mother went to answer it, and there, gaunt and grim-faced as ever, with a cold, severe look in his eye, was P C Simmons. Next to me at the table Ben froze, his mouth wide open and such horror in his eyes that I thrilled with fear on his behalf.

'John's up in the field getting the dip ready, have you time for a cup of tea?' said mother, and then, 'Ben, what on earth are you looking like that for? Go and tell your father that Mr Simmons is here to see the sheep dipped.'

Ben couldn't be frightened like that nowadays, because the police no longer supervise dipping, it's done by a chap from the Trading Standards Department. We didn't have to dip at all for several years, because scab was eradicated in the early fifties, but it came back – some say in a load of Irish sheep in 1973 – and since then we've had compulsory dipping again. Mind you, most farmers would dip anyway, to control all the other parasites.

It's not a popular job with the men, even on a farm as well equipped as Brookfield. The sheep are supposed to go into the dip automatically, but once they've tried it they aren't so keen the second time and a lot of them have to be manhandled. Then they have to be kept in the dip for a full minute, with Jethro laboriously counting the seconds, before being allowed to climb out into the draining pen. By the time they've finished, everybody is smothered in grease and sheep muck and well sprayed with dip mixture.

In my early farming life, we had no dip of our own, but used to hire a wooden bath about four feet long and three feet wide from a chemist in Borchester. It had a wooden draining platform on the side and must have been similar to what Messrs Thomas Biggs were offering in their 1894

143

catalogue: 'Dipping apparatus, £5 and £6; and on wheels £18.'

The bath we hired wasn't on wheels. We had to fetch it with a horse and cart and it took three blokes to operate it – one to catch the sheep and the other two to lift in into the tub, turn it on its back and shove the poor creature's head under. The sheep didn't like it one bit, even when we lifted it out, stood it on the draining board and squeezed as much dip as possible out of its fleece.

We used that method, believe it or not, right up to the mid-thirties, first with P C Simmons keeping a stern and watchful eye on us, then the stout and amiable P C Bates. Then, in 1936, we constructed a permanent dip – and made a mess of it. The dip needed to be five feet deep, you see, but when we were digging it out we struck hard rock three or four feet down and instead of trying somewhere else, I made it where it was, but sticking up two feet above ground. As a result, we *still* had to lift each ewe and lamb bodily and drop it in!

That was a huge success, compared to what we'd been doing before, but I went on getting into a terrible mucky mess. I think I can safely say that I was free of lice, keds, ticks and scab by the time I sank wearily into a bath in front of the kitchen fire, with Doris topping me up with buckets of hot water from the copper.

It was the day that Webber the butler ran amok. I ought to remember it for other things, because it was the first time I went to our village fête as a tenant farmer with my new wife Doris on my arm. But Webber the butler had run amok, and we remembered it forever after because of that.

The fête was held in the grounds of the manor, with the Colonel and Lettie Lawson-Hope presiding. There was red, white and blue bunting strung from the chestnut trees, just as there had been every year since I was a little lad, and tea was served, as always, in the big conservatory, which had an enormous vine and always

144

smelled of moist, rich soil and whitewash. There were the usual attractions and side shows and a 'cinema tent' showing a film about submarines in the First War. You could go for a trip on the lake for a penny, and there were pony rides for the children. The pony, which was normally used to pull the big lawnmower, always wore thick 'socks' to stop his shoes from damaging the grass! For a mere halfpenny you were allowed into the maze. It wasn't quite Hampton Court, but if you played fair and didn't stick your head through the box hedges, it took a long time to reach the middle and find your way out.

The last time I saw that maze was in 1946, when it was showing definite signs of wear. Too many small boys had pushed their way through during wartime fêtes and other fund-raising events and there had been too few gardeners to repair the damage. It looked a sorry sight, patched up with binder twine.

In 1921, though, the year of Webber the butler's great aberration, the maze had hedges that were thick, glossy and green. I'd have gone inside, because it was always my favourite, but Doris wouldn't let me. I was a tenant farmer now, she was a married woman and we were very stiff and proper in our best clothes, wandering around and shaking hands with people. Shrieks of laughter were coming from the maze, and for two pins I'd have taken my coat off and joined it the fun, because I was only twenty-four, after all, and Doris had only just had her twenty-first birthday. But no, we had to stay prim and polite. Doris had been a lady's maid at the Manor up until a few months back and she was worried about her dignity.

By the end of the afternoon I was awfully tired of Doris's dignity, though. She wouldn't even let me roll up my sleeves to shy at a coconut, and when Tilly, one of the young kitchen girls, who was a friendly soul, came and giggled something about me being a fine-looking chap, Doris hissed at her to be on her way before she got a clout round the ears.

All in all I was quite grateful when the afternoon drew

145

towards a close and we gathered under the terrace for the auction of unsold produce. This always happened before the closing speech by the people's warden, in which he thanked the Squire and his gracious wife for yet again allowing us to hold our fête in such a beautiful setting. Colonel Lawson-Hope and his family and guests sat at the top of the steps, the ladies in their long summer frocks and wide-brimmed hats and we villagers gathered on the grass below. The churchwarden, who was Doris's uncle, stood ready to sell off the goods and Webber the butler stood ready to pass them to him.

'Lot number one,' said Mr Forrest, as Webber held it up, 'is a magnificent chocolate cake. Now, what am I bid?'

As he spoke, Webber turned and walked solemnly round the back of the Squire's party and presented the cake to one of the guests. She looked confused, as well she might, and politely declined the cake. Webber insisted. She refused again, this time rather sharply. Webber dropped it in the lap of her white silk dress and walked back to his place next to the churchwarden.

The lady gave a little cry of shock, but nobody quite realized what had happened and the Squire was still smiling benignly as Webber picked up lot number two, a punnet of over-ripe raspberries.

'What am I bid for these raspberries?' cried Doris's uncle, and Webber turned and took them to another of the Squire's party, a middle-aged bespectacled matron, and offered them to her. She refused in some bewilderment so Webber perched the punnet on the top of her large pink hat and walked away.

There was a roar of laughter from the village children sitting on the grass and gasps of astonishment from everybody else. The Squire got up and went quickly through the French windows and into the house. 'I don't believe it,' said Doris, her eyes wide with sheer horror, 'I just don't believe it!' Her dignified afternoon was falling apart, because not only was her uncle being made to look a terrible fool in front of the entire world, but the man doing it was the famous, respectable and all-important Mr Webber, the man who had ruled her with a rod of iron when she worked in the Manor kitchens! All through our courting days – even though she was Lettie Lawson-Hope's personal maid by then – I had to listen to her going on about *Mr* Webber this, and *Mr* Webber that, and many a time she had to cut short an evening and dash back to the servants' hall before Mr Webber locked up.

Meanwhile, the butler had edged his way back to the table and picked up a basket of eggs. 'Look out!' one or two people shouted as he carefully selected one, stared at it thoughtfully for a moment, then lobbed it into the crowd. He managed to throw several more before being led away by a couple of servants summoned by the Squire. After that, the auction carried on again as if nothing had happened with Doris's uncle selling off the chocolate cake, the raspberries and what was left of the eggs!

We all expected to hear that the Squire had found himself a new butler, but he didn't. Webber, it turned out, had been at his master's port, but he was forgiven. The gentry had tremendous power over their staff and tenantry in those days, but it was remarkable how generous they could be when a good servant had a temporary lapse. After all, Webber had been under fire with his master in France.

They used to say that a servant spends the first seven years in a job serving his master, the next seven years serving himself, and the following seven years the master spends serving him. If that is true, Squire Lawson-Hope spent more than his proper share of time looking after old Webber, because he was butler at the Manor until they sold the estate in the fifties.

Our Phil was fuming about Jethro when he called at Glebe Cottage with my milk the other morning. You can usually bet, if there's trouble between them, that it's because Jethro wants to do a job properly and Phil wants him to cut corners. In this case someone had telephoned

Brookfield to say our sheep were out on the road by Foxholes and that there was a hole in the hedge. We were just starting on second-cut silage at the time, and Phil wanted Jethro to nip up and shove a hurdle in the gap, but Jethro wouldn't have it. 'It needs some stakes and a roll of pig netting to do a proper job,' he insisted, 'else they'll be out again, Master Phil, sure as eggs is eggs.'

Phil was in a temper about it, but he gave in because he knew that Jethro was right. The two of them argue, but they respect each other, which is the same with most farmers and their men, particularly those of Jethro's generation. Jethro's the sort of chap who knows instinctively what to do – whether the hay's fit to bale, or if it's too wet to roll a field – and Phil knows he'll always do his best at whatever job he's given.

It's a matter of pride, you see, in a job well done. I'll never forget the terrible indignation among the men the first time we had to 'back-swathe' one harvest at Brookfield in the last war. Back-swathing is unknown nowadays. A modern combine harvester cuts everything in front of it, but the old binder used to cut a swathe at the *side* of the machine. So you always had to scythe a path for it round the sides of the field before it could get to work. Scything was tiring and laborious for the two old chaps helping with the harvest that year and for the women who followed them, binding the corn into sheaves with twisted straw. But nobody complained. It was the *proper* way to do the job and what alternative was there. Trample down a path with the binder and crush all that good, ripe wheat?

Well, that was just what I did. I was desperately anxious to get that field of corn in and there wasn't the time or labour to mess about scything pathways. So we back-swathed. We drove the horses and binder into the crops and cut a swathe round the field – trampling down some of the corn in the process. Then we turned the binder, went back the *wrong* way, and cut the corn we had just run over.

We lost some, of course, but not that much and I was satisfied to have got the crop in before the weather broke, but the men were deeply offended. 'Back-swathing' had saved them from a back-breaking job, but it went against their every instinct to trample down growing corn. You just wouldn't do it, not if you took proper pride in your work.

I suppose it's the stockmen who become the most passionately involved in their jobs. They sometimes behave as though the sheep, pigs and cattle actually belong to them and one of the most savage fights I ever saw was between a cowman and a shepherd who quarrelled over some grass.

I had just taken over Brookfield, a few weeks after my father's death, and I had to go over to Home Farm to see the Squire's cowman about borrowing a bull. When I got there he was just brushing down the yard, having turned the cows out, and we stood passing the time of day, like the true countrymen we were, before getting down to business. Suddenly, the door of the cowshed burst open and out marched the shepherd, sheepdog at heel.

'You get your cows out of that field!' he bellowed, striding towards us.

'Don't tell me what to do wi' my cows,' came the reply.

'That's my grass! 'Tis for the ewes and lambs!'

''Tis for the cows, and that's where they'm a-staying.'

Then it started. The shepherd struck first, without any warning, but the cowman wasn't slow to hit back and in a moment they were going at it hammer and tongs. They were an evenly matched pair, both in their late thirties I suppose, and they were belting away at each other when the cowman's daughter came rushing out of the dairy and leaped like a cat onto the back of the shepherd, clawing his face with her nails till she drew blood. He managed to throw her off and she set up an almighty howl. I was wondering what on earth I could do when the bailiff arrived on the scene, picked up the yard broom, and thrust it between the two struggling men.

It stopped the fight – there was a fair amount of wet cow muck on the end of the broom – and he gave them both a

149

week's notice. It was later withdrawn, though. The bailiff must have decided, on second thoughts, that men who would risk a black eye or bloody nose just to put a few extra gallons of milk into their employer's churn, or a few pounds' weight on his lambs, were men worth keeping after all.

I have known a few rogues in a lifetime as a farmer and more than a few men who were work shy, but the land has been well served, over the years, by the men who have worked it. There are far fewer of them now, of course. In fact, the numbers have dropped so sharply since the last war that there are now more farmers than farm workers and 'mechanization' is generally regarded as the main culprit. I doubt if it's as simple as that though. In the first forty years of my life mechanization made little progress, not because it wasn't available but because it was cheaper to employ a farm labourer and pay him 30s. a week. Nowadays a chap like Jethro is averaging well over a £100 a week, with four weeks' holiday instead of one. So when farm workers retire, or move to take another job, the farmer is often tempted not to replace them. It's as easy to buy a bigger tractor, let the other chaps knock up a bit more overtime and, with luck, make £25,000 or so by selling off a farm cottage.

For the young lads who do come into farming, though, and speed round in their comfortable tractor cabs with endless pop music playing, the prospects are very bright indeed compared to the prospects for youngsters who stood around the hiring fairs when I was a boy. The going rate then was about 7s. 6d. a week for a lad, and he had to pay for his lodgings out of that. My father used to tell the tale of a farmer, the other side of Penny Hassett, who had a reputation for being a pretty tough employer. He had gone to Borchester Fair to hire an under-carter and spotted a likely-looking lad with a bit of whipcord in his lapel – the symbol of the carter's trade. Anyway, they went through the usual preliminaries – where had the lad been working and how much he wanted – and the farmer finally said he would meet him under the clock at half-past two and make up his mind. He then retired to the Drover's Arms and didn't reappear until after three o'clock. The lad was waiting, though, patiently under the clock.

'Ah, there you are, lad,' said the farmer. 'Well, I've been making enquiries about you, and I shan't want you after all.'

To which the youngster is supposed to have replied, 'And I've been making enquiries about you, and I wasn't coming anyway!'

AUGUST

THERE has never been a harvest, so the old chaps in Ambridge used to say, one half as bad as the summer of 1860. It was my grandfather, 'black sheep' Daniel William, who told my father about it when he was just a lad and my father told the tale (which grew, I daresay, in the telling) every New Year's Eve as we sat round the fire in the kitchen. The official tenant at Brookfield in 1860 was still my great-grandfather, Sergeant Benjamin Francis Archer, who was born in 1797 and was a soldier in his youth, but it was his son 'black sheep' Daniel William, who was running the farm. By all accounts it was the most terrible year of his life. Throughout the winter, after the crops failed, the family lived on nothing but 'boiled bread dinner', which was just bread cooked over the fire with a little butter or salt, and a kind of 'Hogs Pudding', which was made by stuffing chitterlings with oatmeal. All the family pride went into keeping old Sergeant Benjamin Francis alive, because everybody thought that it would have been shameful to let 'a man who fought at Waterloo' die of starvation.

They managed it, anyway, because he lasted until 1864, but to get them through that awful winter all the chickens were sold and half the furniture, as well as my grandfather's gold hunter watch and the kitchen clock. The family went for twelve months without knowing what time it was.

It's surprising how little that mattered, mind you. When I was a boy our kitchen clock showed a different time to the one on the next farm. There was no way of checking, you see. The clock in the village shop was the only one reckoned to be right, and that was because folk who went into Borchester were expected to set their watches correctly and come back with the 'right time'.

In 1860, though, the correct time was the least of the problems. The spring was the wettest for hundreds of years and then it rained all through June and the haymaking was the worst in living memory. They were still trying to harvest wheat and barley in October, although it had been so cold that, in spite of all the wet, there was hardly any sprouted corn at all. Root crops failed completely and there was foot rot in the sheep everywhere.

It was when the corn had finally been cut that trouble broke out at Babylon Farm, just over the hill from Brookfield. A man called Ball had the place then and he must have been a rough customer, because the farm still had an evil reputation when I was starting at the village school and I was told not to mix with the 'Ball lads', or else I'd get my ears boxed.

In 1860 Farmer Ball had reason to be in an ugly mood. He'd harvested what corn he could, but then he had to stand and watch while the Parson's men came into the field to take their tythe. They always went into the field once the corn was piled into stooks, and they took away one stook in ten. It was always a bitter thing for a farmer to watch when the harvest was bad and the price of corn was going to be sky high, but in 1860 things were desperate indeed. Farmer Ball and his men stood, helplessly, as the corn was taken away, then they saw that the Parson's men were trying to take one more stook than they ought to have done. That was it. Farmer Ball and his men went in with clubs and sticks and gave them such a beating they didn't recover for six months. Farmer Ball and his family didn't go to church after that and folk said they'd been excommunicated. They hadn't been, of course, but the family's reputation was still under a cloud half a century later.

If the small farmers were badly off at times, things must

153

have been far worse for the labourers and their families. Wives and children used to go out gleaning after the harvest, searching through the stubble for ears of corn that had fallen when the crop was cut. I don't remember it myself, but my mother used to describe how the church bell was rung every morning to tell the gleaners that they could start and to stop anyone having an unfair advantage. People were so poor they'd have been out before dawn otherwise. Then, when the bell was rung, the churchwarden would stand at the gate and announce which fields were ready for gleaning. It wouldn't mean much now, I don't suppose, if Tom Forrest, were to stand shouting 'Round Robin, Wormitts, Pikey Piece', but they're all fields at Brookfield and the village women would have known what it meant a hundred years ago. After the churchwarden had read out his list of fields they'd have hurried to them with their bags and baskets. On the first day of gleaning the women wore clean petticoats for some reason and they'd put the first day's corn in a pile in their bedroom, hoping that it would bring food for the coming year. The giant combine harvester was still and silent. Next to it, at a peculiar angle, were Jethro's tractor and trailer. Our Phil's Land-Rover was on the other side, looking as though it had pulled up in a hurry. Out of the machine were stuck three pairs of legs.

Anyone passing might easily have thought there had been a terrible accident. But, as I supposed, it was another breakdown – and just at the wrong moment when David was desperately trying to finish off the last of the winter barley. The combine had picked up a brick and a fair amount of mess had been caused to its innards before David had managed to turn off the engine. Nobody knew where the brick had come from, unless some idiot had heaved it into the standing corn from the near-by footpath, and there wasn't time to stand around cursing and speculating. Phil raced off to telephone the machinery firm before they knocked off for the night and

I was sent with David to find out if Brian Aldridge could lend us one of his combines to finish the last few acres before the weather broke. He couldn't, as it happened, because his three combines were going flat out, and Phil was just as unlucky. The fitter couldn't get out to us before the next morning, by which time we'd had three or four hours heavy rain.

It wasn't David's fault, picking up that brick, but I'll bet he felt as angry and frustrated as I had done, fifty-odd years ago, when I smashed up the binder in that very same field, and with a very similar storm brewing up over the back of Lakey Hill.

I was getting the last of the oats in then and I felt sure we'd finish in time. The three horses were pulling nicely together, the knotter was working properly for once and the sheaves were being tipped out at regular intervals to be picked up and stooked by Simon and the other chap I had working for me.

We must have made the perfect harvest picture. Then, suddenly, the horses went mad. One moment they were pulling the binder in perfect unison, the next they were plunging about in a frenzy, and a second after that they were heading flat out through the standing crop with me clinging on with one hand and desperately trying to get the binder out of gear with the other. I didn't manage it, though, because I was instantly surrounded by a horde of angry wasps stinging like fury, and as I struggled to beat them off and haul on the reins the sails of the binder, which were turning at three or four times their normal speed, were knocked off one by one.

The horses had disturbed a wasps' nest and the wasps had taken their revenge. As the storm cloud rolled towards us from a yellow, thundery sky, I could do nothing but send the binder off to the wheelwright's shop, take a regretful look at my oats and go home to bathe my stings.

Wasps don't cause many problems these days. They can't send the engine of a combine harvester wild with panic and the driver's safe inside his cab, with its green-tinted windows and its air-conditioning, but when I was young they were a constant menace. Once I was scything round a field of wheat with old Josh, not long before I took over Brookfield; one moment he was swinging away with that easy rhythm of his, which I always envied and never managed to achieve, and the next he had dropped his scythe, clapped his hands over his head and was running towards the Am with a swarm of wasps behind him. It takes a lot to make a sixty-year-old take a ducking, but those wasps did it for Josh!

The binder was a machine that cut the corn and tied it up into sheaves and it was in general use on farms for about sixty years until the combine overtook it in the fifties. It was a very ingenious invention and didn't change much in design from the first machine to the last. You can still see them occasionally, on farms where they produce straw for thatching (it's no use trying to thatch with straw from a combine), but they're pretty well redundant, really. The binder could cut the corn and tie it into sheaves, but those sheaves then had to be put into stooks to dry and finish ripening. The stooks then had to be carted and built into a rick and later the rick had to be pulled apart and the corn threshed and put into sacks. Finally, the sacks had to be hauled into the granary.

The combine harvester pretty well does the lot. It cuts the corn, threshes it, shoots the grain out into a trailer and throws the straw out at the back. Jethro or Neil drives the trailer back to the grain store or drier, where Phil tests the moisture from time to time and keeps any eye on things.

Neither weather nor wasps are as feared as they were – but there is always somebody to throw a brick in the machinery, and there is always plenty of room for human mistakes. About ten years ago, we took on a student to help with the harvest at Brookfield and he got into terrible bother. He was completely inexperienced, but he fancied himself on a tractor seat and he proved better than Jethro at keeping the trailer under the grain-spout while the combine was moving. One afternoon, though, he hauled a load of wheat back to the buildings, smiling and thinking himself no end of a fellow while at the same time, the trailer was gently tipping three or four tons of grain out in a neat swathe across the field behind him. He had accidentally moved the lever of the hydraulic lift – an easy enough thing to do, I suppose, but Jethro teased him mercilessly for the rest of the time he was with us.

Few of us can afford to laugh, though. When I was eight or nine I thought *myself* no end of a fellow. My usual job at harvest time, when I got home from school, was to take the cider out for the men, carrying it in a little barrel on a chain. The men shared an old horn mug and we allowed them a mugful apiece after every load (they were allowed as much as they wanted at the end of the day, mind you). My next job was to move the horses between the rows of stooks, shouting out 'hold tight!' in my high-pitched voice for the benefit of the chap on the wagon who was building the load. I had pleaded, several times, to be allowed to take a load back and one afternoon my wish was granted. There were two horses, one between the shafts and a lead horse hitched on in front, and the carter would walk alongside and shout 'come back!' if he wanted the lead horse to go left, or 'gee back!' if he wanted it to go right.

'Now make sure you don't let him turn too short,' the carter warned me, as I left the field with my precious load, ''cause if you do you'll have the load off sure as anything.'

That was exactly what happened. As I was turning into the rickyard, I mixed up my 'come backs' with my 'gee backs' and the lead horse turned too short, the front wheels locked, and over went the wagon.

'Who the devil let young Dan bring that load down?' roared my father, as everyone rushed up to put things right. Fortunately, there was no real damage, but I didn't discover that until later. Fearing my father's anger, I had fled into the house in tears and was safely in bed by the time he came in.

* * *

Old Matthew Partridge was what they call a 'character'. He kept a dog and a pig and at night, the three of them would sit before the hearth in Matthew's cottage, and Matthew would scratch the pig's back and wish that someone would scratch his. Parson Woodbury was a 'character' as well, by all accounts a very humorous sort of character, because when Matthew's granddad died, in the late 1800s, Parson Woodbury composed an epitaph for him that says:

> Oh death! Fie, fie!
> To kill a Partridge in July!

And it was Parson Woodbury who is supposed to have made up the epitaph on the grave of two brothers:

> Here lie Paul and Richard Fenn,
> Two lawyers, yet two honest men.
> God works miracles now and again.

I suppose there have always been one or two 'characters' in the village, with each generation. Walter Gabriel bought two elephants called Rosie and Tiny Tim back in the early sixties, so I suppose that made him a 'character'. We had a chap at Brookfield when I was young who might have qualified – he certainly did some daft enough things. My father was sorting out piecework rates for hoeing some mangolds one day, and there was disagreement as to how wide the field was. 'I'll pace it out,' said Dad, but Geoff Parker, the chap I'm talking about, insisted that *he* should step it out and he did so, walking over to the far hedge with carefully measured tread.

'Well?' demanded my father, impatiently, when Geoff had slowly walked back. 'How many yards was it then?'

'I dunno,' replied Geoff, 'I didn't count.'

Perhaps Geoff was just not as clever as he might have been, but he had the wit to get himself a job as Squire

Lawson-Hope's chauffeur in the twenties. I met him on the Hollerton road once, leaning against the Squire's Bentley in the sunshine, wearing his yellow and tan uniform and quietly smoking his pipe. It was soon after 'pneumatic' tyres had come in, and the Bentley had a puncture.

'Oh Lord,' I said, 'how are you going to deal with that?'

'It ain't too bad,' said Geoff puffing away unconcerned. 'It's only the one tyre that's flat arter all, and that 'un's only flat at the bottom.'

Every August we have our Flower and Produce Show, and every year, when I walk into the village hall and smell that unmistakable, mingled scent of flowers, fruit, dust and vegetables, I think of an amazing 'character' called Marge Dagg, who got herself into terrible trouble at the Ambridge Flower Show of 1937.

The show itself doesn't change much. One year there'll be a marvellous display of runner beans, ramrod-straight after having weights cunningly hung on them while they were growing, and the next year, the weather'll be bad for beans and there'll be just a few miserable specimens. The basic pattern's the same, though, and I reckon I just about know the schedule off by heart. 'Potatoes, kidney, 4, one variety; Peas, 8 pods, one variety; Gladioli, 3 spikes; Asters, 5 blooms, any variety or colour in a vase. . . ' and so on, with classes for cakes, jams and chutneys, a handicraft section which varies from year to year – this time there was a class for corn dollies – and always something for the children, usually handwriting and a wild-flower arrangement.

The only new class to have made its appearance since the last war is 'Home Made Wines', and very popular it is too, and the only thing to have disappeared is the 'set tea' that was once such an important feature, with trestle tables groaning under mountains of bread and jam, potted-meat sandwiches, scones and cakes – and all for 9d. a head back in the 'good old days'. I'll never forget settling down on one of the benches for a tuck-in with Phil and Jack when they were both young, and Phil embarrassed me something awful by piping up in a voice that carried the length of the tent, 'But *why* have I got to eat till I'm ready to burst, Dad?'

That, then, is our Flower Show, the event that always reminds me of old Margery Dagg and her cauliflowers.

Marge had a few acres scattered on the far side of the village from Brookfield, and lived in a small and rather overgrown house with an 'off-licence' that nobody ever seemed to patronize. How she made a living was a mystery as her only form of income seemed to come from three or four old cows. These she used to drive to a paddock near her house every day and milk them as they stood without bothering to tie them up. Some folk said the poor old cows were too frail to move. At other times, Marge was seen trundling an old pram about with anything inside it from a truss of hay to the week's groceries. She wasn't what you'd call *popular* – she kept herself too much to herself for that. If a newcomer took pity on her and asked her in for a cup of tea, Marge would reply that she never took tea with anyone except Mrs Lawson-Hope. As it probably never occurred to the Squire's wife to ask Marge up to the manor, we assumed she never went out to tea at all.

In fact, she never went anywhere except to the Flower Show. The W.I., the church fête, whist drives, and socials in the hall at Christmas all had to get along without her, but once a year she changed her dirty tweed coat and faded hat for a flowered frock, went down to the field behind the village hall and regular as clockwork won the prize for the best cauliflowers. Others could fight over the onions and marrows, the carrots and the beetroots, but when it came to caulis there was never a doubt who would win. Nobody knew how she managed it, year after year, and nobody could find out because her garden was too overgrown with brambles and rhododendrons to see into.

In 1937 it happened again. We all herded into the

marquee after the judging and, sure enough, there was the red prize with 'Mrs Dagg' written on it, in copperplate handwriting, by the show secretary, Mr Creech. Then came the prizegiving. 'Cauliflowers – Mrs Dagg' bawled out Mr Creech, who was really our village baker and was enjoying his afternoon of authority.

You'd never have recognized Marge as the person usually seen prodding her ancient cows along the lane behind the village. Now she positively flounced up to the table, a huge smirk on her face as if to say, 'I could wipe the board at the W. I. show too, if I wanted!'

Mrs Lawson-Hope gave her a white envelope containing two half-crowns. 'Congratulations, Mrs Dagg,' she said, not for the first time, 'I really don't know how you manage it, year after year.'

'Well I do!' bellowed a voice from the crowd and Tom Hilder, who used to have Bank Farm just beyond Marge's place, elbowed his way up to the table waving a cauliflower's root and stem in either hand. 'I found these stumps this morning in my field, back of Mrs Dagg's house. I'll bet anyone a guinea they fit her exhibits.'

And they did, perfectly. 'There you are,' shouted Tom in triumph, 'I've always grown caulis but I wouldn't enter them here. It wouldn't be right.'

Well, some folks gasped with shock, others were too surprised to do anything, and some of the young folk clapped and thought it was no end of a lark. Marge, though, just walked straight out, her head held high in the air and her prize money clutched to her bosom. And she never came back, which suited Walter Gabriel because he had won every class but cauliflowers over the years, and in 1938 he got his red prizewinner's card for them at last.

Old Marge Dagg might have been a bit of a cheat – but she was a real character!

The corn harvest is always said to be the crown of the farming year but it is by no means the only job at Brookfield during August. The usual routine with the pigs keeps Neil busy four or five hours a day and however frantic they are to get the wheat and barley harvested the baconers still have to be sent off, and the piglets weaned, and the sows put to boar. The cows still have to be milked twice a day, although this is probably the slackest month of the year in the dairy and a lot of cows will have dried off ready for calving. In fact, the first calves will start to arrive by the end of the month. Graham often takes his holiday early in August, when the rest of the farm is bracing up for frantic activity, because things are quiet in his particular department.

The tail end of the lambs will be going off fat, and those that aren't fit for slaughter may well be sent off to market for sale as 'stores' – that is, lambs somebody else will buy and fatten, perhaps on some roots. Phil's usually had enough of lambs by August and is pleased to clear them out in one go rather than fiddle about farming a few at a time.

Then there's the potatoes to keep an eye on. They need spraying regularly with a fungicide to make sure they don't get blight. And once a crop of corn is brought in the stubbles have to be cleared and cultivated ready to start the cycle all over again. Gone are the days when the stubble could be left for Michaelmas geese to wander over, fattening themselves day by day on the spilt corn. Now Phil's in more of a hurry than ever, because he's growing oilseed rape and needs to get fifty acres of the early winter barley stubble ploughed and worked down and ready for drilling before August is out.

The surprising thing is that although August is the main harvest month, the combine harvester is still standing idle for more days than it is actually working. A modern average-size combine can deal with twenty acres a day if conditions are right, and we only grow about 250 acres of cereals at Brookfield – so in theory it could whiz through the lot in less than a fortnight. But conditions *aren't* always right. One day, with a cloudless blue sky, a hot sun beating down and the combine greased up ready to go,

Phil will be out there, rubbing an ear of corn and chewing a grain or two. Then he'll shake his head. The corn just isn't ripe. A few days later the corn's ready, but drizzly rain is falling from a grey sky.

The combine just has to wait until the sky is clear, the corn is ripe, and the dew has lifted. Then it comes into its own, eating up those twenty acres and justifying its £40,000 cost.

I sometimes wonder how we managed to harvest at all in the old days. I suppose we just kept cutting, sometimes when it wasn't ready and sometimes when the dew was on it, and hoped it would ripen out in the stook. Sometimes it did, but often it didn't and we'd be out there turning the sheaves to stop them sprouting, knocking the stooks down and remaking them – anything, in fact, to get them dry enough to carry to the rick. Messing about with wet sheaves, by the way, is one job that's guaranteed to soak you through to the skin. We used to tie thick sacks round our waists and try all sorts of devices to keep dry, but none of them worked. One chap who worked for me in the thirties, cut up an old cycling cape and tied it round his legs and body, looking like a Michelin man, but the water soon found a way through. Another problem was the length of straw. We couldn't spray it with chemicals to keep it short, the way we do nowadays, and sometimes wheat straw would be five feet long, and if it was full of thistles, which it often was, your hands got so full of the blessed things that there wasn't room for any more.

I often think it's a peculiar thing that they invented hormone weedkillers, which just about did away with thistles overnight, at exactly the same time combine harvesters came into general use – which meant we didn't have to handle sheaves anyway!

The first sign of winter often comes, curiously enough, on a still morning at the end of August, when the mists are lying along the meadows by the river and the sun rising with the promise of a hot summer's day. The corn will

163

have been cut, and from the stubble-fields of Trefoil or Midsummer Meadow I will see figures on horseback moving towards the kale in Skipperley and hear the excited cries of young hounds. 'Cubbing' has started, and the November meet at The Bull suddenly seems very close indeed.

Cubbing isn't really designed simply to kill foxcubs – whatever the hunt may say. Its main purpose it to *teach* young fox hounds that they *are* allowed to chase foxes. They wouldn't dare do it otherwise, you see, because ever since they were sent on farms to 'walk' they have been taught *never* to chase after cats, ducks, sheep, dogs or any other livestock.

So, late in August, when the corn is cut and the vixen leads her young into the root crops, the hunt arrives and the hounds are loosed. To help them, the field is surrounded by members of the hunt on horseback and on foot, who try to turn back any foxes attempting to escape.

Many do escape, of course, and just as the hounds are taught their lawful prey, so the agile fox cubs are taught their greatest enemy. To a countryman the arrival of the hounds after the harvest means that although one season on the land is drawing to a close, another season is soon to begin.

SEPTEMBER

'FRESH COWS' MILK – D. Archer, Brookfield Farm, Ambridge' said the engraved brass plate on the side of my seventeen-gallon churn, and I stood proudly by it, ready to ladle out milk to the housewives and parlour-maids of Borchester, and looking *extremely* neat in my new breeches, stiff collar and tie, and bowler hat.

Why we had to dress up in that fashion I can't think. Customers associated the purity of the milk with the cleanliness of the milkman, naturally enough, but it was a real palaver getting that stiff collar and tie on every morning, and keeping my bowler in position when it rained and I had to wear an oilskin over it.

It was in September 1929 that I first put the horse into the trap, loaded up a churn of milk and set off to sell my wares in the suburb round the Edgeley road. I felt terribly self-conscious, and when I drove past Bridge Farm the whole Atkins family stared at me open-mouthed, then ran to the hedge and gave me a cheer. Piggy Atkins had the place then. He'd taken the tenancy because it was practically being given away, and that morning he was burning great piles of squitch with Rosemary and their four children helping him.

I don't know why but every time Mr Fletcher over the road is burning squitch from his vegetable plot (he suffers terribly from the stuff) and I smell that distinct, acrid tang I'm carried back to that mellow September morning fifty-odd years ago, when Rosemary was raking up the squitch and saw me perched up on the trap wearing my bowler hat, and burst out laughing. She'd been one of the Wynyard 'beauties' when she was a girl and she was still a remarkably handsome woman. Her children were as handsome as she was, all with that same chestnut hair and those big eyes, not a bit like Piggy Atkins, who was a notably ugly man. One of those lads, by the way, is still sticking pigs round Ambridge and Penny Hassett even though he shouldn't. He must be one of the last, mind you. Modern hygiene and welfare laws have outlawed private pig stickers and the old farm pig benches are turning up in antique shops. Peggy bought one awhile back, to use as a garden table.

In 1929 Piggy Atkins was trying his hand at farming, which was a daft thing for him to do because farming was in a very bad way indeed. We livestock men never suffered to the extent of the arable farmers over in the east, but we had a struggle to pay our way. The post-war farming 'boom' petered out in the early twenties, you see, and we all had a grim time after that.

For the Archer family, ill-fortune started with the final illness of my father, who collapsed in the summer of 1923 and was in and out of hospital for the next year. Overnight, I found myself having to run two farms, and the larger of them, Brookfield, was in a pretty sorry state. My father had been unwell, old Josh had retired, and the bloke who had been taken on in his place was good for nothing. Mother wouldn't let me sack him – 'Your father will be back in a week or two', she kept saying – and I just had to run things as best I could. For a year, I had to get two herds of cows milked each day and make sure two lots of corn were drilled and hoed and harvested. Frank was long gone; he'd left in 1919, on a passage to New Zealand paid for by the Salvation Army, who also gave him an outfit and farm training when he got over there. It was a scheme aimed at poor lads from the city slums and Frank shouldn't have been allowed on it. Dad was very bitter to think one of his sons was going round the other side of the world to be given 'farm training', but Frank never really intended to be a farmer. It was the adventure he was after, the excitement of travel to faraway places. He must have

166

had a lot of Archer blood in him, though, because he ended up farming sheep near Christchurch, just about 'down-under' from my flock on Lakey Hill.

In August 1924 my father died, and Doris and I, with young Jack, moved back to Brookfield. We were sorry to leave Weston Farm, which had been our first home and where our first child had been born. I had farmed my few acres with growing skill and my mistakes had been covered up by my enthusiasm. Even in that final year, when I finished work every day only to hitch up a horse and get stuck-in at Brookfield, I was thoroughly happy and blindly confident. I was only twenty-seven, you see, and a lot more proud of myself than I ought to have been.

We moved at Michaelmas, 29 September, and that night Doris made a fire in the kitchen at Brookfield. My mother sat on one side in her usual place and I found myself having to sit on the other side in my father's old pine chair, which had a devilish uncomfortable cushion full of lumps. I read the paper, which was still full of J. B. Hobbs, 'Surrey's hero', and Herbert Sutcliffe of Yorkshire and the marvellous things they'd managed against Australia. My mother did her knitting and Doris sat at the table working out her egg-and-butter account. There's a lass in Ambridge now, Clarrie Larkin that was, who married Eddie Grundy and moved to Grange Farm. She's got a little boy about the same age Jack was when we moved to Brookfield. I called at Grange Farm for some reason a few months ago, and Clarrie was sitting by the old range they've got with William on her knee. She reminded me so much of Doris I stood staring in confusion, and she made me sit down and drink a cup of tea with brandy in it.

Clarrie has quite a hard life, I think, but she's a good-hearted capable girl and so, thank God, was my Doris. Because when I settled down at Brookfield and took stock of the situation I realized that things were looking very black. September was the month when farmers made an annual contract to sell their milk to a dairy, and the price

I'd been forced to settle for that year was dangerously low, The dairies were in a powerful position, you see. Our cows had to be milked twice a day whatever happened and the milk had to be sold immediately because there was no refrigeration. The buyers from the dairies knew this and bargained ruthlessly. In London, the National Farmers' Union tried to get some order into the market by agreeing a price with the wholesalers, and local groups of farmers tried to do the same. Heaven knows, prices were low enough – something like 5d. a gallon for summer milk and a bit more for winter milk, if you were lucky. And for that we had to put it on the railway twice a day.

It was 1929 before I took the plunge and decided to retail my own milk. The past five years had been the toughest of my farming life. At Weston Farm I had worked long but satisfying hours to build my own farm, but the depression was beginning to hit hard. At Brookfield, I learned how different it was to work long, back-breaking hours just to fend off bankruptcy. Doris was working as hard as I was and we didn't dare think of having another child for five years after Jack was born.

In September 1929, I went to the farmers' meeting in the back room of The Feathers in Borchester and sat round the table with Jess Allard, Fred Barratt and a couple of dozen others. The Feathers wasn't so posh in those days, it was an old coaching inn with stables where we farmers could leave our horses. Before the meeting everyone was agreeing that we couldn't accept less than 6d. a gallon, but by the time the meeting was over, we had come down to 5½d., but not a farthing less! The next day, though, we heard that several farmers in the meeting, including the chairman, had signed contracts for 5d. a gallon.

That finished it. I can remember storming in to Doris and telling her that from now on we were going to market our own milk and the dairies could go hang. She looked terribly startled, poor girl, and not without cause. She knew that anything I couldn't sell on my milk round – and

168

I hadn't even *got* a milk round – would have to be made into butter or cheese by her. She looked for a moment at our Phil, who was just old enough to toddle round the kitchen and cause havoc, then at our Jack, who had just come in with a basket of eggs he'd collected, then she gave me a little smile and said, 'All right. If that's what you think best.'

I certainly didn't *want* to spend two or three hours a day hawking milk round from door to door, but I didn't believe I had any choice. There was no money in corn and no profit in milk at the price we were being offered. So the following Saturday, I set off to Borchester on my bike. I had settled on the middle-class area growing up on our side of town, just off the Edgeley road, and began knocking on doors. Once again, I found myself in a buyer's market. There were any number of folk, either local dairies or farmers like myself, willing and eager to deliver milk to the doorstep. I could see I'd have to undercut everybody else by at least a halfpenny a pint, and that was what I did, as well as assuring potential customers that my milk was fresher and creamier than anyone else's. By the end of the day, I had enough names and addresses in my little book to make it worth a try, and the followng Saturday I put a churn of milk in the tap, a bowler hat on my head and set out.

And so, for the next few years, I was a milkman. Every morning after milking I had my breakfast, changed into my smart clothes, and off I went with one or two seventeen-gallon churns, a covered bucket to carry from door to door and measures of different sizes. One tip I learned from an old hand was to pretend to give folk a little extra. First I'd ladle their pint, or quart or whatever, then I'd dip the measure back into the bucket – not far enough to pick up any milk, mind you – then I'd up end it with a flourish into their jug. I became quite an expert at diverting the customer's attention with a weather prediction or an enquiry about their little child's latest ailment.

On a sunny day in spring or autumn I used to enjoy being a milkman, getting away from the farm for a couple of hours and meeting people. But it was a dreary business in winter, driving the trap along icy roads to Borchester, then going from door to door ladling the milk with frozen fingers. And it wasn't very much fun in hot weather, what with the flies and customers complaining that the milk was 'off' when it wasn't anything of the kind.

I don't think I made a bad milkman, all in all. I was soon selling Doris's butter and cream along with the milk and it was a proud day when I was confident enough to fix a brass plate with my name and the name of my farm to the side of one of the churns.

I wasn't sorry though when, in 1933, the Milk Marketing Board was set up and farmers were guaranteed, a fair price for their bulk milk; neither was Doris. I'll never forget the way she had to bustle round the dairy in those days, sometimes with Jack working the butter churn and young Phil turning the handle of the cream separator and little Chris crawling on the floor, getting in the way.

Nowadays, Mike Tucker is the only farmer in Ambridge who has a milkround – and it's a far cry from the sort of job that I took on! He drives round in his Japanese pick-up, delivering milk to customers and he doesn't even bottle it himself any more. The bulk tanker collects his milk, the dairy drops a supply of bottled milk at his farm every day and at the same time collects the empties. No wonder he was whistling when I saw him the other morning!

Neil was stubble cleaning in Coombebell, his bright red tractor crossing and re-crossing the hard, yellow ground. Along the hedge, by Foxholes, he disturbed a covey of partridge and they fluttered up and skimmed over the hedge into Marney's out of harm's way.

I was pleased to see them, because partridge have been a rarity at Brookfield for many years. We grubbed out many of the hedgerows they used to nest it, you see, and when they tried to nest in the fields of grass, we chopped their nests and eggs and young birds to pieces with our forage harvester. Those that survived to their first winter found little to eat because we had ploughed to stubble the fields, and the spilled grain was not there to be gleaned.

It wasn't only us, of course. We've been very 'conservationist'-minded compared to a chap like Brian Aldridge. Modern farming methods brought about the decline of the partridge just at they wiped out the corncrake and endangered cowslips. The only consolation for the grey English partridge is that, although the shooting season starts officially on 1 September, most landowners leave them be for another month and many refuse to shoot them at all.

It was a different matter when Tom Forrest stepped into my father-in-law's shoes and took up keepering. Partridge were plentiful and he was forever chasing round the stubble fields after poachers. Partridge don't roost in trees like pheasant, but like to 'jug' together on the ground, usually facing outwards in case of attack by foxes. Tom reckoned that poachers came during the day, wandering along the footpaths as innocent as you like, but really looking to see where the partridge were 'jugging'. In the thirties, he was forever stalking after parties of hikers who came across the fields in their shorts and boots singing, 'Merrily, merrily, life is but a dream' and songs by George Formby. One year he went prowling after a courting couple and the chap blacked his eye and reported him to P C Bates. Everybody laughed at poor Tom, but the poachers were real enough and they did come back at night, towing nets across the stubble fields on long drag cords and dropping the net when they heard the partridge flutter. In the end, Tom and the other keepers started putting hawthorn twigs out in the fields and they fouled the poachers' nets up.

Nowadays the stubble fields aren't with us long enough to be used by partridge or poachers. As soon as a field is cleared of corn the stubble-cleaning tackle goes in. The idea is to kill the weeds and encourage weed seeds to germinate, so they can be ploughed in out of harm's way. You can control weeds later with chemicals if need be but it's an expensive business and the cleaner your fields are to start with the better.

Most years we are still harvesting corn well into September, although we do sometimes finish in August. In 1983 we had most of our winter corn drilled before September was out. 'My old dad would turn in his grave,' I said to Phil, 'if he could see you sowing wheat before October. Oats maybe, but never wheat!'

'Blow your old dad for once!' Phil said. 'It might rain all next month – and the month after that. I'm going to bash on!' I must say I didn't blame him.

There are plenty of other jobs to be done in September. Phil likes to get the muck spread before it gets too wet, and some hedges trimmed if there's time. The cows are still out at grass day and night, but calving is getting into full swing.

Phil used to go in for something called 'steaming up', which basically meant feeding the cow more and more cake as she got near to calving in order to increase her milk yield. It worked, of course, and sometimes the udder got so big you had to start milking the cow several days *before* she calved and store vast quantities of this special, colostrum-rich milk in the fridge ready to give the calf. Meanwhile, a lot of cake had gone into making a big calf, so we tended to have more trouble when it came to calving. 'Steaming-up' was a daft idea and I never altogether agreed with it, but our Phil was determined to follow the fashion and we had fifteen years of difficult calving before he saw the light.

Mind you, calving is far from straightforward these days and the danger of milk fever is never far away. Milk fever is caused by too much of the cow's calcium going into the calf or the milk. It can usually be cured by an

172

injection – and the recovery can be dramatic. One moment, Graham has a freshly calved cow lying helpless in the loose box, looking just about ready for the knacker, and half an hour later she's up on her feet eating a scoop of nuts.

Over in Marney's and on Lakey Hill Phil and Jethro will be looking at the sheep this month, going through the entire flock inspecting their teeth and udders. These are the crucial parts of a ewe; they enable her to feed herself and to feed her lambs. Unless she can do both jobs properly there's no room for her at Brookfield.

For the first four years of a sheep's life, its teeth are developing and you can judge its age fairly accurately. Then it becomes 'full-mouthed', and after that it starts to deteriorate. Once it starts to lose teeth, Phil decides to get rid of it. If it's all right in the bag – in other words it hasn't had mastitis in one 'quarter', so it can still feed two lambs – he sells it at Borchester market for breeding. If its udder is bad, it is sold for slaughter.

Out of 300 ewes Phil will have lost ten, perhaps, during the course of the year and he will cull another sixty or so. In September, seventy yearlings will be bought in from up north.

We used to have Cluns and I always looked forward to attending one of the big sales on the Welsh borders early in September every year and buying in our replacements. I felt quite cheated when Phil changed over to 'mules', which are a cross between the Swaledale ewe and Bluefaced Leicester ram. Instead of taking me for a day to the sale, he gets someone to produce his replacements for him in Cumbria and they simply arrive by lorry.

Those were the days, when we used to drive our sheep to Borchester and home again on foot! It sounds like something out of Thomas Hardy, I know, but it went on until well after the last war and, at this time of year, it was nothing to see four or five lots of lambs being shepherded along the back roads to Borchester market.

It was fine as long as your sheep were 'settled' and you

had a lad to run ahead shutting gates and blocking gaps in the hedgerows, but once your sheep were frightened and got their heads up, it became the very devil of a job. I've had sheep running across fields and mixing themselves up with other flocks. I've had them in the river and I remember once a sheep jumped a wall and broke its neck. (On that occasion I startled the woman in a near-by cottage by rushing in and demanding a carving knife. She obviously thought I'd escaped from an institution, but I just wanted to bleed the lamb and, at least, save something from its untimely end.)

The worst journey of all, though, took place after I'd bought a bunch of ewes at Borchester and engaged Billy Watson to help me get them home. Billy was a well-known character at Borchester market, who made a living of sorts by helping the auctioneers and taking on the odd bit of droving. I arranged to meet him at the market office at three o'clock and went off to do my other business. At three, I was ready and waiting. At half-past three I was getting very irritated indeed. 'Try the Drover's Arms', I was advised. I did, and there was Billy, as tight as an owl.

'Shorry, boss, I'm jusht coming . . .' he said, fixing me with a bleary eye while his friends manfully tried to help him to his feet. They managed it, but the moment they let go of him, he promptly sat down again.

'Shorry boss,' he said sadly and I just nodded and dashed out of the Drover's Arms and back to the market. I was too late. The usual gang of hangers-on had disappeared. The market was empty, except for my pen of ewes and my sheepdog bitch, Muff, who was tied to the rails. I looked at my sheep thoughtfully. They looked quiet enough. Perhaps Muff and I could manage them between us?

Five minutes later and we were out in the High Street, with me in front and Muff bringing up the rear. My ewes were as quiet as I could hope for and a couple of chaps helped when they looked like turning into West Street.

174

They didn't even take alarm when an old lady waved her arms violently to stop them going into Underwoods. In no time at all we were out of Borchester and taking the back road to Edgeley and Ambridge, and I thought I was home and dry – and what was more, I'd saved the pound I was going to pay Billy!

Then disaster struck. A vicious-looking dog, on a long, rattling chain shot like a bolt out of a cottage porch barking and snarling for all he was worth. He couldn't get among the sheep, but they didn't know that. One moment I had a quiet bunch of ewes and the next they were everywhere.

It took me and Muff a good ten minutes to get them together and after that it was trouble, trouble all the way to Brookfield. Every gap in the hedge was an invitation – and there were plenty of gaps because gypsies were in the area for potato picking and they needed wood to keep their fires alight. It took us over two hours to reach Edgeley, and when we got there my ewes found a garden gate open and I was pelted with rotten apples by the 'lady' of the house while I did my best to get them away from her sprouts and broccoli. An hour later, just as it was starting to go dark, I finally, and very wearily, turned them into the track at Brookfield. Perhaps having ewes delivered by lorry is a better idea, after all!

Mr Fletcher was red in the face and very angry-looking and Joe Grundy was shaking his head from side to side disapprovingly.

'Here, Dan,' he said, 'have you seen that black and white house in Glebelands then?'

'There aren't any black and white houses in Glebelands,' I said, falling right into the trap, 'they're all modern.'

'Well mine's black and white!' Mr Fletcher suddenly burst out and thumped his pot down on the bar loudly. 'It's been black and white ever since Brian Aldridge set fire to his straw!'

'Your granddaughter's husband,' said Joe, looking at me accusingly, 'ruined poor Derek's paintwork – ruined it.'

Mr Fletcher, it seemed, had been painting the big expanse of weatherboard across the front of his house with best white gloss when suddenly the air filled with black smuts.

'What would happen if I did that sort of thing at my works in Felpersham?' he demanded, glaring round the bar. 'If I let so much as a puff of smoke escape I've got the authorities round in no time at all. Yet you farmers fill the sky with smoke, cause accidents on the roads, pollute people's swimming pools, burn the hedges – and completely ruin my paintwork.'

'Not all farmers,' said Joe, 'only the irresponsible ones. It's shocking behaviour though.'

Joe doesn't burn his straw. He doesn't make all that much and his cows, calves and turkeys use up quite a bit. 'I'm an old-fashioned chap,' he said, 'and I think the best place for straw is mixed with muck and ploughed back into the land.'

I had to agree with him about that, whatever the 'research stations' and 'experts' might tell us. But Brian Aldridge has more than a 1,000 acres of cereals and oilseed rape, and only a small herd of beef cattle to use the straw up on. He couldn't turn it all into good manure even if he wanted to. He tried selling it baled 'in the field' to a Welsh hill farmer once, but the chap didn't turn up for it or pay for it and, in the meantime, Brian couldn't get into the field to plough. Then the weather turned wet and the stuff was still sitting out there in the spring. Brian had to sow barley instead of winter wheat and claimed he lost a lot of money.

Mind you, he's made enough profit out of cereals lately – and that's part of the straw-burning problem. There's more cash in cereals than in livestock and farmers have been forsaking horn for corn. Then again the corn itself is thicker as yields have risen, so there is more straw being

176

produced on every acre. When I was a lad, the high spot of harvesting was chasing the rabbits as they bolted out of the last bits of corn in each field, but we hardly ever see a rabbit in the corn nowadays. It's partly because of myxomatosis, of course, but if you ask me the straw is just so dense now that the rabbits can't live and move about in it anyway.

They reckon there's six million tons of straw each year that nobody seems to want and most of that's produced in areas like East Anglia, where there's not much livestock to use it up on. They've tried turning it into building boards, they've tried treating it with chemicals to feed to animals, they've tried compressing it into briquettes for fuel, but nothing makes much of a dent in those 6,000,000 tons.

I tried explaining some of this to Mr Fletcher, but it didn't do much good. 'You're just saying that straw is the waste product from a highly profitable business enterprise,' he said, 'but the farmers aren't prepared to spend a small amount disposing of it in a responsible manner. The more money they get the more greedy they get. They've become arrogant, smug and selfish, and don't care a damn about anybody or anything but themselves!'

We don't hear that sort of thing in The Bull very often, and even Sid, behind the bar, looked a bit shocked.

'Some of that may be true, Derek,' said Joe, cautiously, 'but always remember that some farmers are different from others.'

'And I won't argue with that!' I said, relieved to be able to agree with somebody about something. 'Now, can I buy you all a drink?'

I bought a round, and then Mr Fletcher insisted on buying me a pint because he was sorry he'd been het-up, and it was going dark before I left The Bull and walked back down the village to Glebe Cottage. In the distance, though, beyond St Stephen's and the Am, I could see

Brookfield and the bright lights of a combine bobbing slowly across Long Field, where David and Neil were working late to get the last of the wheat in, I thought of old Ned Larkin when he was young Ned Larkin, drinking cider after haymaking back in the thirties, and saying as how a chap at Felpersham cut his grass by night using electricity and Simon Cooper telling him not to be such a daft beggar. Then, because of what we'd been talking about in The Bull, I suppose, I suddenly remembered something that happened when I was a lad and hadn't thought about in years. It was the end of the harvest at Brookfield, and while my father and his men were carting the wheat, I was messing about at the side of the field with Silas Winter and Walter Gabriel. One of them pulled half a cigarette out of his pocket – Walter, I daresay, because Silas smoked a clay pipe from the age of seventeen – and somehow, before we'd managed more than a puff of cigarette each, there was a crackling sound and flames were spreading through the stubble. We jumped up and tried to stamp them out, but there was a bit of a wind and we didn't stand a chance, so I yelled to Josh, who was up on the load, and he slid down and ran over shouting, 'Quick, boy, get the wagon up the other end of the field.' Then he and the other two chaps set about the flames, and finally managed to put them out.

We lost about twelve stooks, and when I looked round for Silas and Walter they had vanished. I was alone, a small and very frightened boy, as my father, who had been building the rick down in the yard, came striding across the field towards me.

Eighty years ago! I walked up the path to Glebe Cottage, past the tall, orange dahlias planted by Doris when we 'retired' from Brookfield, and, d'you know, I could almost feel my bum smarting from the tanning my dad gave me with an old stirrup leather on that September afternoon when I first got into trouble for burning straw.

INDEX

Aldridge, Brian 6, 59–60, 171, 175; *see also* Home Farm (today)

Aldridge, Jennifer 59

Aldridge, Kate 59–60, 107

Allard, Dick 101

Allard, Jess 93, 131

animals, wild 41, 48–9, 55, 63–5, 72, 82, 84, 96, 111; *see also* rabbits

Archer, Ben 98; as child 3, 21, 39, 71, 108, 116, 117, 141–3; family farm work 19, 72, 82, 128;

Archer, Sergeant Benjamin Francis 5, 152

Archer, Chris 9, 65, 87–8, 170

Archer, Daniel (Dan) 79–81, 83, 98, 157; as child 1–9, 19–23, 41–4, 88, 107–8, 115–7, 155; farm work 71–3, 81, 127–8, 133–6; life with Doris 7, 11–13, 46, 90, 109, 114–5, 137–8, 144, 145–6, 167; as milkman 165, 167–70; wars: South African 2; World War I 7, 32–3; World War II 31–3; Weston Farm 97–102, 167, 168; *see also* Brookfield, middle period

Archer, Daniel William 4, 20, 124–5, 152

Archer, David 13, 58, 81, 129–30, 138; cows 10, 20, 28–30, 42, 49–51, 61, 105–6; crops 9, 113, 127, 129–30, 154

Archer, Doris 11–13, 17, 47, 114–5, 143; farm work 27, 30, 32, 64, 65, 66, 67, 68, 87, 106, 132, 167–70; life with Dan 7, 46, 90, 108–9, 137–8, 145–6

Archer, Elizabeth 57, 138

Archer, Elizabeth Harriet 2–5

Archer, Frank 2, 72, 97, 98; to 128 New Zealand 166–7

Archer, Jack 27, 71, 87, 114, 160, 167, 168, 170

Archer, Jennifer 59

Archer, Jill 10, 30, 63, 67, 86

Archer, John (Dan's father) 5, 88, 97, 119, 123–5, 178; family life 1–9, 19–21, 41–4; farming 72–8; illness and death 34, 45, 83, 98, 99; *see also* 166 Brookfield, early

Archer, Mrs John (Dan's mother) 45, 75, 76, 77, 98, 100, 119, 127, 166; family life 1–9, 19–23, 38–44

Archer, Peggy 59

Archer, Phil 42, 63–5, 71, 109, 147; as child 9, 71, 106, 160, 169, 170; *see also* Brookfield today

Archer, Shula 22, 31, 80, 93, 108, 109, 138

Archer, Tony 6, 9

Art (roadman) 108

Ashfield 7, 113

Atkins, George 2

Atkins, Piggy 137, 165–6

Atkins, Rosemary (née Wynyards) 47–8, 117, 137, 165–6

179

Babylon Farm 153
badgers 48–9, 65
Badger's Bank 9
Barratt, Fred 7, 67–8
Bates, P. C. 131–2, 141
beer and ale 20; Temperance
    Movement 57, 128
Biggs, Messrs Thomas 140, 143–4,
birds 40–1, 55, 56, 63, 65, 75, 84,
    89, 95–6, 115, 170–1
Blower family 32, 135; Joe 120,
    126; Sam 108, 110
body, in hay rick 131–2
Borchester 4, 43–5, 56, 74, 150,
    152–3, 165, 168–9; market 40,
    41, 173–5
Bowen, Godfrey 137
Bridge Farm 6, 9, 165
Brookfield (house and
    buildings) 7, 10, 46, 58
Brookfield early 6–10, 38–9, 51–3,
    73–6, 79–81, 118–9, 152;
    accounts, office work 60–1,
    123–4; harvest 71–3, 126–7,
    128–9; sheep 134–7, 140; see
    also 143–4 Archer, John
Brookfield, middle period (Dan
    and Doris) 58, 59, 66–8, 123,
    139, 166; crops and harvest: 71,
    76, 119, 120, 148, 154, 163; hay
    126–32; dairy work 49–52, 105–6,
    112, 165; sheep 86–8, 136, 140–4,
    173–5
Brookfield today 7–10, 35, 61–2,
    79, 112–4, 123, 139–40, 170; cows
    and dairy work 13–14, 28–30, 42,
    49–52, 80–1, 106, 112–3, 162,
    172–3; crops and harvest 11, 85,
    112, 121, 139, 154, 161, 163; hay
    and silage 126–7, 130–1; office
    work 57–60, 81; pigs 19, 81, 92–5,
    112, 162; potatoes 12, 102, 162;
    poultry 66–8; sheep 5–6, 7,
    78–81, 86–7, 113, 148, 173, 174;
    to market 113, 140, 162, 174;
    shearing 134–7
The Bull 31, 33

'bull in a bowler hat' 61
Burminton Hovel 54

Carter, Neil 102–3; farm work
    42, 62, 79, 81, 127, 134, 170;
    pigs (at Hollowtree) 19, 81,
    92–5, 113, 162
Carter, Susan 25
carting 32–3
church 11–13, 30–1, 141, 153
cider 25, 27–8, 75, 157
Collard, Graham 14, 28, 30, 42,
    81, 162
Cooper, Simon 49, 61, 64,
    132–3, 155
Cow Pasture 78, 131
cows, dairy work 8, 9, 10, 13–14,
    21, 49–52, 61–3, 70, 76–7,
    80–1, 105–6, 112, 139, 162–70;
    calving 28–30, 103–5, 172–3;
    sales 91–2
Creech, Mr (baker) 161
cricket 116–7
Crook, Miss (shopkeeper) 107–8
crops, cereal passim, 10, 24,
    31–2, 72, 78, 113, 120–1, 139,
    171–2

Dagg, Margery 159, 160–1
Danby, Colonel 30
darning sacks 82
Davis (head keeper) 47
dogs 7, 41, 54, 86, 87, 96, 174–5;
    foxhounds 23, 89, 164

farm sales 89–92, 100
farming innovations,
    mechanization 15, 15–18,
    119–20, 127, 139–40, 150
Fields, Pat 48–9
Five Acre 42, 83, 113
Fletcher, Derek 25, 31, 37, 74,
    116, 117–8, 165, 175–6
Forrest (Tom's father) 146
Forrest, Doris see Archer, Doris
Forrest, Tom 22, 65, 69, 79, 83,
    115, 118, 171

foxes 66; hunt 8, 21–3, 75, 89, 164
fruit 2, 12, 75, 77, 139

Gabriel, Nellie 91
Gabriel, Nelson (Walter's father), and family 1, 26, 54, 56, 116–7, 142
Gabriel, Walter 8, 91, 158, 161; as child 1, 17, 26, 54–6, 88, 108, 110, 111, 178
geese 162; goose grease 44
gleaning 153
Glebe Cottage 67, 75, 99, 177
Glebelands 25, 74, 175
Grange Farm 28, 167
Grating, 'Bony' 131
greasing carts and wagons 82
Grundy, Clarrie, and William 167
Grundy, Eddie 25
Grundy, George 46, 91–2, 110, 117
Grundy, Joe 13, 25, 27, 31, 37, 74, 116, 117–8, 126, 175, 176
Grundy, Ted 31

hares 65, 96
harvest 148–9, 152–7, 161–3, 177–8; Harvest Festival 11–13; hay 33–4, 126–32, 153, 176–8
hedgehogs 15
Hickman (farmer) 43
Hilder, Tom 161
Hollerton 76–7, 89, 101, 110
Hollowtree 8; pigs 81, 92–5, 112, 162
Home Farm today 6, 12, 15, 34–5, 54, 58, 78, 84, 97, 113–4, 120, 123, 132, 136, 149, 155, 175–6
horses 16–17, 22, 34, 64, 76, 100–1, 128, 144, 155; dealers 89–90

'Jack in the Green' 115
Jenkins (coachman) 88

Josh 8, 20, 39, 51, 52, 71, 72, 77, 82, 83, 97, 156, 166, 178
Judge, Mr (at Bull Farm) 47

keepers, game- 40–1, 48, 50; see also Forrest Family

labour 42–3, 58, 100, 102–5, 139, 141, 149–51, 154, 158; pay 73, 98, 127, 150–1
Lady Day 89–90, 99
Lakey Hill 6, 9, 83, 94, 112, 137
land girls 103–5
land sales 89–90, 99, 124–5
Larkin, Clarrie 167
Larkin, Jethro 85, 94–5, 102–3, 129, 143, 147; work 5–6, 62, 78, 115, 127, 131, 140, 156–7
Larkin, Lizzie 137
Larkin, Ned 41, 73, 133, 178
Lawson-Hope, Colonel (Squire) 17, 34, 40, 41, 55, 88, 89, 99, 144–6, 160
Lawson-Hope Estate 6, 89, 99, 146
Lawson-Hope, Lettie 3, 11, 144–6, 160

Marfurlong Farm: sale 90
Marney, Joseph 7
Marneys 134, 170, 173
May Day, Old 115
Meadow Farm 91–2, 124–5
Michaelmas 89, 102, 167
Moss, Charlie, and widow 99
Mumford (undertakers) 56

Netherbourne, Lord: his father 89
New Year's Day 57–8, 59–60
Nobbs, Ricky 111

oilseed rape 10, 70, 114–5, 139, 162
'Old Carrots' 91

Parker, Geoff 158–9

181

Parsons (farmers) 91–2
Partridge, Matthew 158
partridges 89, 170–1
Penny Hassett 16, 46–8, 117
Perkins, Mrs, and Arthur 59
Perks, Sid: at the Bull 24, 31, 117–8
pests 14, 112, 118–22, 139; sheep dip 140–4
pheasants 40–1, 84
pigs 19, 25–7, 92–5, 166; see also Carter, Neil
plants and wild flowers 3, 13, 69, 84, 105–6, 112, 122, 137, 163
ploughing 16–18, 101
poachers 33, 40, 171
potatoes 14, 32, 101–3
poultry 66–8; egg-collecting 19–21, 75

rabbits 24, 40–1, 75, 100, 133, 177
raddling 5–6, 78
rats 55–6, 65, 72, 82
reading rooms 55–6, 57
Reed, Tommy 110
'Rook and Rat' clubs 55, 56
rooks 75, 95–6
Rosie (land girl) 103
Rutter, Sergeant 33

Sabbath Day: work 119
sayings, rhymes 3, 11, 23, 38, 39, 95, 118, 158; farming 10, 25, 27, 32, 63, 83, 84, 95, 105, 116, 118, 136; weather 25, 45, 69, 70, 81, 83–4, 122
sheep 5–6, 7, 10, 63–5, 78–88, 173–5; orphan lambs; 80–1, 86–8; shearing 134–7; sheep dipping 140–4
shooting 75, 89, 171
shows, fairs, fêtes 36, 43–5, 115, 141–3, 159–61
Simmons, P. C. 141, 142, 143
Simms, Elizabeth Harriet (Mrs

Daniel William Archer) 2–5
Simms, Josiah, and family 4–5
Smart family 8, 73
songs and singing 46–7
spraying, fertilizing 15, 112, 118–22, 139
Stan (labourer) 122
stone-picking 103–5
stubble fields 24, 162, 171–2
Styles, Nobby 135
sugar beet 34–6
Sunny Dingle 9
superstitions 3, 21, 39, 137, 153; see also sayings

Ten Elms Rise 6, 23, 81
threshing 8, 71–3
Tregorran, Carol 12, 110
Tring, Zebidee 108
Troutbridge farm 23
Tucker, Mike 170
tythes: of harvest 153

vegetables 14, 31–2, 74, 75, 110, 160–1
vicars 13, 22–3, 57, 111, 117, 153

wars: South African 2; World War I 7, 31, 32–3, 76, 86, 97, 98, 99, 147; World War II 31–3, 102–5, 121, 147
wasps 155
Watson, Billy 174
weather 1, 9, 12–13, 14, 63–5, 81, 83, 153; see also sayings, rhymes
Webber, Mr (butler) 11, 144–7
weeds 77, 119–20, 122, 163
Weston Farm 97–102, 167, 168
Whipple, Sammy 59, 116, 136
Whipple, Tom 46, 47, 117
Wynyard, Polly and Rosemary 46, 47, 117, 137, 165
Wynyards Farm 27–8